BENJAMIN FONDANE'S
ULYSSES

Judaic Traditions in Literature, Music, and Art

Harold Bloom and Ken Frieden, *Series Editors*

Benjamin Fondane's
Ulysses

BILINGUAL EDITION

Translated from the French and with an Introduction
by Nathaniel Rudavsky-Brody

With a Foreword by David Rieff

Syracuse University Press

First Edition 2017
17 18 19 20 21 22   6 5 4 3 2 1

∞ The paper used in this publication meets the minimum requirements of
the American National Standard for Information Sciences—Permanence of
Paper for Printed Library Materials, ANSI Z39.48-1992.

For a listing of books published and distributed by Syracuse University Press,
visit www.SyracuseUniversityPress.syr.edu.

ISBN: 978-0-8156-3499-7 (hardcover) 978-0-8156-3516-1 (paperback)
978-0-8156-5399-8 (e-book)

Library of Congress Cataloging-in-Publication Data
Available upon request from the publisher.

Manufactured in the United States of America

supported with grant
Figure Foundation

in assay goes sanity

Contents

Foreword

DAVID RIEFF

A horrific death at a young or relatively young age is like a powerful acid dissolving the meaning of everything that had come before in a life. The person who dies so terribly may not have lived for most of his or her time aboveground in a worst of all possible worlds, though surely this is at least sometimes the case. But that is likely to be how his or her contemporaries perceive the thing, while those who come later are even more vulnerable to such a "rewriting." Kierkegaard's wise and in most cases commonsensical adage that "life must be understood backward . . . [but] must be lived forward" does not apply here. Instead of the writer's life and work being more understandable in retrospect, the manner of his or her death becomes the "star of the show," consigning the life, however avidly and richly lived, and the work, no matter how valuable, to a place further down in the credits. It must be a biographer's nightmare, in the sense that Adorno meant when he wrote that "Horror is beyond the reach of psychology." The actual life and death, and the literary afterlife of the poet, filmmaker, critic, and philosopher Benjamin Fondane, who was born in Jassy (Iași) in Moldavia in eastern Romania in 1898 and was murdered in the gas chambers of Auschwitz-Birkenau in October of 1944, is a poignant illustration of an artist's end overshadowing all that came before, as if the two principal meanings in English of the word *end*, which are "conclusion" and "goal," had somehow become conflated.

Fondane was born Benjamin Wechsler in 1898, the second of three children. His father, Isaac, was a prosperous businessman, and his mother, Adela, was a member of the Schwarzfeld family, which counted among their number several distinguished intellectuals, notably Fondane's maternal grandfather, Benjamin Schwarzfeld, who founded the first Jewish school in Jassy, and his uncle Elias, who was the author of a history of Jews of Romania. Fondane's career as a writer began early. While still in secondary school, he was already being published under the pseudonym of B. Fondoianu. By the time Fondane was out of his teens, he had published a number of well-received translations into Romanian of Yiddish poetry, writes articles for a number of Jewish magazines and newspapers both in Jassy and in Bucharest, as well as poems of his own. But it is *The Breaking of the Stone*, a short play written in 1918, that established Fondane's reputation among the thriving world of avant-garde intellectuals and artists in Bucharest.

Fondane abandons his studies after three years at the law school of the University of Jassy and moves to the Romanian capital in 1919. He continues to write poetry and criticism, but takes a job as an editor at the Zionist daily *Mantuirea*. It is the era of the three-cornered debate within the Jewish world in Romania between Theodore Herzl's Zionist nationalism, the cultural Zionism of Ahad Ha-Am, and of course religious Orthodoxy.[1] Inevitably, Fondane is caught up in the debate but does not explicitly take sides between Herzl and Ahad Ha-Am. As the Fondane scholar Carmen Oszi has written, despite Fondane's prominent role as a writer and commentator, he remains somewhat detached from the debate, "oscillating between utopianism and pragmatism, between [his] desire for a [Jewish] spiritual renaissance and [Zionism's] territorial aspirations." As for Zionism, fascinated as he is by it, Fondane sees it "not

1. Bundism, the anti-Zionist socialist movement that is so strong in Poland between 1918 and 1939, does not have the same importance in Romania.

as a break with traditional Judaism but as a newly emerging form of it."[2]

Even during this early period of his career, Fondane is engaged in projects and with subject matter in which Judaism, let alone Zionism, play no role. In 1921, alongside his elder sister, Line, who was an actress, he founds "The Island," an experimental theater company in Bucharest modeled on the work of the French director Jacques Copeau, founder of the Vieux-Colombier theater company, above all on Copeau's repudiation of the boulevard comedies that dominated the establishment French theater of the period, and which had been taken up in Romania as well, which was hardly surprising as Romanian intellectuals and artists had always looked to Paris for inspiration. Fondane shared this Francophile orientation, the difference being that it was the France of the avant-garde rather than of the boulevards that enthralled him. Fondane himself is very clear about this. In 1922, he publishes a volume of essays on various French writers. In the preface to the book, he asserts that Romanian literature is a de facto dependency of French literature. It is a stance that earns him the enmity of many Romanian writers, above all on the extreme nationalist Right, though given the ferocious anti-Semitism of that movement, and its rejection of the idea that Jews could be considered Romanians at all, a view that alas is all too explicit even in the early work of E. M. Cioran, though he would later become a friend and declare himself an admirer of Fondane's, presumably anything he wrote about Romanian culture would have been rejected out of hand. "The Island" was short-lived, failing after a little more than a year, both for financial reasons and because of these predictable anti-Semitic responses. To claim that Fondane decided to leave Bucharest and settle in Paris because of these racist pressures would be an overstatement. Nonetheless, the failure of "The Island" seems to have hastened that decision.

2. http://www.benjaminfondane.com/un_article_bulletin-Benjamin_Fondane _et_le_d%C3%A9bat_sioniste_en_Roumanie-23-1-1-0-1.html.

Arriving in Paris in 1923, Fondane hits the ground running. While he continues to write articles in Romanian for a number of avant-garde journals in Bucharest, he also accomplishes what many scholars but only a few creative writers have ever done successfully,[3] adopt the language of his adopted homeland. The Romanian-language writer B. Fondoianu becomes Benjamin Fondane, and from then on, his important work, whether in philosophy, criticism, cinema, or poetry, would be in French. As it had been in Jassy and Bucharest and would be for the rest of his life, both in France, where settled, and in Argentina, to which he made two long trips in the 1930s, first in 1931 to present a cycle of avant-garde films and then again in 1936 to make a film, *Tararira*,[4] Fondane's productivity was nothing short of Stakhanovite. A year after his arrival in Paris, two crucial events in Fondane's life occur: his sister, Line, joins him, and he meets the émigré Russian philosopher Lev Shestov, whose intellectual disciple Fondane becomes. From then on, Fondane will assume the motley both of the philosopher and of the poet and literary critic. If one goes down the list only of the criticism he published between 1925 and 1935, one finds on the literary side essays and reviews about René Char, Jean Cocteau, Jacques Copeau, and Céline, as well as debates both in print and in person with the major figures of the surrealist and Dadaist movements, notably André Breton, with whom Fondane had an intense if uneasy relationship. In 1930, he finishes a

3. The stellar example of this in English is Conrad. In France in the twentieth century, apart from Fondane the only other important examples are Cioran, who abandoned Romanian for French when he arrived in Paris in the late 1930s, and Beckett, who began to write in French during the same period but continued to write in English as well.

4. Fondane's work in Argentina, both as a filmmaker and in collaboration with *Sur*, the most important cultural journal of the period, and his friendship with *Sur*'s founder, Victoria Ocampo, are well described in an article by the great contemporary Argentine author and filmmaker Edgardo Cozarinsky, published in the Buenos Aires newspaper *La Nacion* in 2006 (unfortunately, there is no English translation). See http://www.lanacion.com.ar/817360-benjamin-fondane-en-la-argentina.

book-length study of Rimbaud.[5] A book-length study of Baudelaire, *Baudelaire et l'experience du gouffre* (Baudelaire and the Experience of the Abyss), remains unfinished at the time of Fondane's deportation to Auschwitz. On the philosophical side, apart from numerous articles Fondane writes about his master, Shestov, he also produces pieces on Kierkegaard, Heidegger,[6] Husserl, Bergson, and Freud. In 1935, these pieces are collected and published under the title *La Conscience malheureuse* (The Unhappy Consciousness).

And Fondane the poet: what of him? From his first efforts as a schoolboy in Jassy, Fondane's focus seems to go back and forth between philosophy and poetry. But while he did not abandon Romanian prose, he does seem to have considered his career as a Romanian poet to have ended with the collection called *Landscapes* that Fondane published in 1923. In a new preface he wrote to that volume in 1929, Fondane wrote that "the present volume belongs to a poet who died around 1923 at the age of twenty-four." And then Fondane adds: "dead? No, murdered."[7] But over the course of his life in France, that is, in the twenty-one years between his arrival in France in 1923 and his deportation to Auschwitz in 1944, Fondane writes five volumes of poetry in French. These are *Ulysse* (Ulysses), published in 1933, the volume appearing here in Nathaniel Rudavsky-Brody's brilliant and admirably faithful translation; *L'Exode* (The Exodus), written in 1934 and like *Ulysses* reworked during the war; *Titanic*, published in 1937; *Le Mal de fantômes* (The Sorrow of Ghosts), the last poem of which was written in 1943; and finally *Au temps du poème* (In the Time of the Poem), which Fondane was still working on at the time

---

5. Shades of Proust, the book, which is called *Rimbaud le voyou* (Rimbaud the Thief), is turned down by the great French publisher Gallimard.

6. The title of that essay, "Sur la route de Dostoyevskï" (Along the Path of Dostoyevsky), could have applied just as well to Fondane's own work, though a Dostoyevsky refracted through Shestov, and counterbalanced by Kierkegaard.

7. I owe this point to the brilliant preface written by the brilliant French Fondane scholar Henri Meschonnic in *Le Mal des fantômes*, the definitive collection of Fondane's poems in French that was published by Éditions Verdier in 2006.

of his arrest and deportation. Where to situate these in Fondane's body of work?

Writers and critics are much given to speculating about what work will "last" and what will not, though one wonders whether Fondane with his Pascalian (more, I think, than existentialist) obsession with absence—the absence of God, of course, but also the absence of any possibility of transcendence, whether secular or religious—would have found such parlor games of any great interest. What he did believe, which we know because he expressed it so forcefully in an essay comparing the roles of poetry and philosophy that he published in *Cahiers du Sud* in 1935, was that, as he put it, "to the lamentable resignation of the philosopher, [the poet] opposes a permanent threat of new acts, and with them the looming possibility something far stronger. [The poet] is a dispenser of life whereas the philosopher dispenses death." Just as, for the great English poet W. H. Auden, "all art aspires to the condition of music," for Fondane "all distilling of thought, every passionate expression, cannot when all is said and done take any other form than that of the lyric."[8]

Fondane's privileging of poetry is hardly dispositive. Writers, after all, are often not the best judges of their own work, and the more realistic among them can really only hope that, as it were, something in what they have written finds a reader after it leaves them. This is part of what Nadine Gordimer meant when she remarked that "one must write as if one were already dead." In the case of Fondane, though, nothing so existential is required. Rereading his poetry, criticism, and philosophical writings in the second decade of the twenty-first century, his criticism, while often discerning, is very much of its time. He is no Gide or Valéry. And his philosophical work, while more substantial, at least when judged by the highest standards, is finally of the second rank. As a Dostoyevskian, he is no Shestov; and as an existentialist, he is no Camus or Sartre. But in his poems, there is everything

8. Benjamin Fondane, "L'Esprit et le temps: La Conscience malheureuse," *Cahiers du Sud*, no. 171 (Apr. 1935).

he knows, but also myths artfully retold and daringly transformed, particularly in *Ulysses*. Fondane's Jewishness fuels his reimagining of Ulysses's voyages as that of the wandering Jew—"A Jew," he writes, addressing Ulysses, "naturally you were a Jew." But Fondane's Ulysses is also the figure of every immigrant, "carrying his life in his suitcase." In his refusal to accept his own destiny, Fondane's Ulysses is the avatar of Camus's *homme révolté*, unreconciled to the world and refusing even the consolation that resignation and acquiescence to one's destiny might afford.

It was this Fondane, great poet and great soul, who choked to death in a gas chamber in Auschwitz. But to make the horror of his death the focus is to grant the Nazis their victory. Better to look to a life profoundly and passionately lived, and to work that mattered then and matters still. Begin here, with *Ulysses*.

Acknowledgments

Of the many people who helped me with this translation, I am particularly grateful to Michel Carassou, Fondane's literary executor and editor, for his extensive aid; to Monique Jutrin for sharing her knowledge and invaluable reference materials; and finally to Olivier Salazar-Ferrer for his judicious feedback and meticulous corrections of the final manuscript. Any remaining errors are, of course, my own.

I owe a debt of gratitude to the Susan Sontag Foundation for its generous support as well as to the Maison de Poésie d'Amay and its director, David Giannoni, and director of residences, Pierre-Yves Soucy, for granting me a month of calm that allowed me to devote myself fully to this remarkable poem.

Finally, I would like to thank my friend Karim Benslama for his patient rereading of earlier drafts of this translation.

Publication Acknowledgments

All quotations from Benjamin Fondane's works appear courtesy of Michel Carassou, Fondane's literary executor.

The two unnumbered opening poems also appear in *Passageways*, edited by Camille T. Dungy and Daniel Hahn (San Francisco: Two Lines Press, 2012), 26–35.

Poems I and II also appear in *Two Lines Online*, http://www.ca translation.org/volumes/passageways.

Poem XXXVII also appears in *Cinepoems and Others*, edited by Leonard Schwartz (New York: New York Review of Books, 2016), 44–47.

Translator's Introduction

In his last letter from the internment camp at Drancy in the spring of 1944, Benjamin Fondane gave his wife, Geneviève, instructions for the final selection of his poetic works, which he had left as piles of manuscripts at the time of his arrest. By the time the long poem *Le Mal des fantômes* (*The Sorrow of Ghosts*) appeared in the October–December issue of *Les Cahiers du Sud*, Fondane was dead, having been deported to Auschwitz-Birkenau that summer and sent to the gas chambers on the second of October. After the war, news of Fondane's death brought an outpouring of eulogy from his friends and colleagues. His work, however, fell into neglect in the years that followed (Geneviève withdrew to a convent and took religious vows), and the collected poems, as specified in that last letter, were definitively edited and published only in 1980, some thirty-six years later.

What reemerged was the striking voice of a poet who had navigated an independent path through the literary and philosophical currents of 1930s Paris. It was a voice shaped by a series of significant personal translations. Fondane was born in 1898 in Iaşi, capital of the Romanian province of Moldova and center of the region's thriving Jewish community. His maternal grandfather was a leading figure of the Haskalah, or Jewish Enlightenment, in Romania, and Fondane was immersed in both Yiddish and German cultures. Yet his debut as a young writer was in Romanian—and Romanian literature, as Fondane himself was the first to point out, was steeped to the point of subservience in French. "I did not know French literature as

I might have known German literature," he wrote in the preface to a 1922 volume of his early essays, "—I *lived* it."

Fondane spent a few years at the center of Bucharest's literary avant-garde, and with his sister, Line, and her husband, Armand Pascal, he founded the city's first experimental theater, Insula. The success of their theater was short-lived, however, and in 1923 the three moved to Paris in search of wider horizons. Yet expatriate life for Fondane was no movable feast; the two decades he spent there were a time of unremitting and unromantic precariousness, struggling to support himself through a series of thankless jobs, first in an insurance office, where he met his wife, Geneviève, and later as a low-level scriptwriter for Paramount Studios.[1] He devoted years to mastering his adopted country's language, bent on reinventing himself in French. Until that mastery was achieved, he wrote little poetry and published even less. Still, he actively participated in the intellectual life of his new city and acted as a conduit for the French avant-garde toward Romania through his articles for the magazines *Unu* and *Integral*.

Fondane's critical position was marked by his diffidence toward the surrealist movement. From the start, he criticized André Breton and his followers for making a moral imperative of automatic writing and found their ideological commitment to Marxism deeply misguided. The mistrust was mutual, and in 1930 Fondane and Breton even came personally to blows during the famous literary brawl at the Maldoror. Yet Fondane held the earlier Dada movement, led by his fellow Romanian Tristan Tzara, in high esteem for having wiped clean the literary slate. Surrealism being Dada's self-proclaimed successor, though, he was not insensitive to the siren call of its language. He participated in several "dissident" surrealist publications, and his first significant poetic text in French, *Three scenarii: Cine-poems* (1928),[2]

1. His one credited contribution was as screenwriter for Dimitri Kirsanoff's *Rapt*, with music by Arthur Honegger.
2. Recently translated by Leonard Schwartz in *Cinepoems and Others*.

is also his only work with an unambiguously surrealist tenor. These unfilmable screenplays are purely literary works, but they reflect Fondane's enthusiasm for the work of Man Ray and Luis Buñuel, whose version of surrealism was the only one to which he could wholeheartedly subscribe. In 1929 Fondane was invited by the grande dame of Argentinean letters, Victoria Ocampo, to present the films of these two artists in Buenos Aires.

The long poem *Ulysses* was the result of that voyage, which Fondane made aboard the steamer *Mendoza*.[3] Fragments first appeared in magazines in 1930,[4] and in 1933 the full volume was published by *Les Cahiers du Journal des Poètes* in Brussels. This first version of the poem contains the basic elements that would come to define Fondane's entire poetic oeuvre through its central trilogy, *Ulysses—Titanic—The Sorrow of Ghosts*, and most of the autobiographical material from his childhood that makes for some of the poem's most evocative passages. Here already is the superimposition of the mythical wanderer Ulysses on the figure of the wandering Jew and of Ulysses's voyage on the modern Atlantic passage; here already is the conflation of the desperate refugees fleeing the Ukrainian pogroms of 1903, whom Fondane had seen as a child, with the streams of emigrants seeking new lives across the ocean. Though less articulately expressed than in later versions, here already is the incurable estrangement of life as a cultural and linguistic exile and perpetual outsider: as a Jew in Romania, as a Romanian in Paris, and as a poet with an unquenchable thirst for life amid the dulled masses of modern society.

The *Ulysses* of 1933, however, was to be profoundly reworked a decade later, in the dark period 1941–43, to become the poem we know today. These revisions bear the heavy stamp not only of the

3. Operated by the Société Générale des Transports Maritimes à Vapeur, with regular ports of call in Genoa, Marseille, Almería, Las Palmas or Dakar, Rio de Janeiro, Santos or Montevideo, and Buenos Aires.

4. For instance, Paul Valéry and Léon-Paul Fargue's *Commerce* and the dissident surrealist magazine *Le Phare de Neuilly*.

German occupation and the uncertainty of Fondane's situation as a Jew in hiding, but also of the years that separate the two versions of the poem and add successive layers of experience and reference. Images of Fondane's 1929 voyage have been doubled by his second voyage to Argentina in 1936 aboard the *Florida*, where he returned to direct the ill-fated film *Tararira*. (Deemed too absurd by its commercial distributors, *Tararira* was never released, and the last copies were lost after the war.) These references have been teased out by literary historians:[5] the "little Breton teacher closed in her shell" (XVIII) is Georgette Gaucher, a promising young poet who had been posted as a French teacher to Montevideo and whom Fondane met on the crossing and with whom he pursued a furtive affair and close friendship during his six-month stay in Buenos Aires; diary entries of Dutch journalist Ernst Claes confirm that the *Florida* indeed encountered "panting fog" (XXIV) after passing the mouth of the Rio de la Plata; the regular and irregular Spanish ports of call that Fondane had visited in 1929 were bypassed in 1936, their silent coasts offering no commentary on the battles between Republicans and Fascists raging inland; Italian poet and Fascist sympathizer Giuseppe Ungaretti (XXVII) found himself aboard the *Florida* returning from the Fourteenth International Conference of the PEN Club.

Yet even when it does not lapse into biographical gossip, this historical reconstruction can give a false impression of reestablishing with too much certainty the relationship between the poet's raw material and his poetic process. A poet of Fondane's temper needs to be read in good faith. The poem's most moving sections—and it is no disservice, given the desperate circumstances of its second composition, to point out that it is at times an uneven poem—are the ones where personal recollection and allusion are subsumed in a poetic movement that transcends the individual references.

5. See the articles by Namenwirth, Nirenberg, Escomel, and Jutrin in the bibliography.

More germane is the observation that the poem's language has been cleansed of much of its remaining surrealist character. This move reflects Fondane's definitive rejection of surrealism, as worked out in his critical works *Rimbaud le voyou* (Rimbaud the Hooligan, published in 1933) and *Faux traité d'esthétique* (Fake Treatise on Aesthetics, 1938) and continued in his last critical work, *Baudelaire et l'expérience du gouffre* (Baudelaire and the Experience of the Abyss, posthumously published in 1947). Individual references to the surrealists still remain, such as the double noun "panic beauty" (VIII), which recalls Breton's "joie panique" or "panic joy," but the poem's intertextual depth comes as much from its echoing of classic figures of French literature—Charles Baudelaire, Arthur Rimbaud, Paul Valéry—as from Fondane's engagement with his contemporaries. Most significant of the development between the first and second versions, however, is the noticeable sharpening of the poem's philosophical focus, for those intervening years saw Fondane's transformation from a poet grasping at broadly philosophical questions to a frankly philosophical poet and indeed an apprentice philosopher.

That transformation, which represents the last and perhaps most significant of Fondane's defining personal translations, was several years in the making, and elements are already present, though tentatively, in the *Ulysses* of 1933. The key figure here is Lev Shestov. When Fondane met Shestov at the salon of Jules de Gaultier in 1924, he was surprised to learn that the Russian philosopher was still numbered among the living, having devoted a series of articles to one of Shestov's books a few years earlier in the belief it was a classic from the previous century. For several years their relationship remained superficial. In 1927, however, Fondane wrote Shestov a letter in reaction to the recent French translation of the book *Dostoevsky and Nietzsche*, a letter in which the philosopher perceived the sign of that rarest kind of reader: one who had understood what was really at stake. In his commemorative essay on Shestov, "By the Shores of the Ilissos," Fondane recalls having written that "if tragedy and misfortune were the conditions for the search for truth—and that was indeed his argument—who would follow him deliberately? Who would dare wish tragedy on himself, even in exchange for the beautiful eyes of liberty? Never, I said, will you have a disciple."[6] Yet Fondane was to become that disciple. One of his most moving works was to be the collection of letters and notes from their discussions that he confided to Victoria Ocampo's safe-keeping on the eve of the war and that was published only in 1982 as *Rencontres avec Léon Chestov* (Meetings with Lev Shestov).

Shestov took it upon himself to train his young friend, in his own philosophy, of course, but especially in the writings of his sources and his adversaries, guiding him through readings of Hegel, Kierkegaard, Nietzsche, Husserl, and Heidegger. With Shestov's encouragement, Fondane began publishing articles on these figures and soon was given responsibility for a column titled "Living Philosophy" in the important Marseille-based literary review *Les Cahiers du Sud*. He came to be viewed as Shestov's representative, and his main philosophical works—the collection of essays *La Conscience malheureuse*[7] (1936) and the posthumous *Le Lundi existentiel et le dimanche de l'histoire* ("Existential Monday and the Sunday of History")—are expositions and developments of the master's struggle. Shestov's thought can be described only as a struggle, against the evidences of reason, the comfort of all too coherent philosophical systems, the resignation of contemporary thought before the tyranny of technical and social progress. Fondane and Shestov, for instance, were delighted by philosopher Lucien Lévy-Bruhl's ethnographic report that members of primitive societies were not burdened with the law of the excluded middle and could affirm two contradictory propositions with perfect intellectual integrity. The serpent in the garden of modernity was none other than reason itself:

6. "Sur les rives de l'Illissus," in *Rencontres avec Léon Chestov*, 28 (my translation).

7. The translation of this title as "The Unhappy Consciousness," following the standard rendering of Hegel's phrase "unglückliche Bewußtsein," seems to me as unsatisfactory for the French as it is for the German. Something along the lines of "Wretched," "Misfortunate," or "Ill-Fated" would be more appropriate.

July 16, 1935

The other day Boris de Schloezer[8] and Mme Bespaloff[9] found themselves at the home of Gabriel Marcel. They both pointed out that in his latest book, *The Broken World*, there were clear traces of Shestovian thought. Marcel acknowledged this:

"This book has been written for several years. At the time, I was overwhelmed by Shestov's thought. But eventually I came to realize that he was knocking at a false door. And later still, that where he was knocking there wasn't even a false door, but no door at all."

Shestov: This comment of Marcel's is not lacking in finesse. Yet had he been willing to see, he would have noticed that this discovery of his was also offered by my writings. I have done nothing but tirelessly say and repeat exactly that, that there is no door, and nevertheless one must knock at that door that does not exist. "Knock, and it will be opened to you," say the Gospels. But they do not say, knock at such a place, at such a thing; it is clear that if we were given a door, if we saw that door, we would knock there: the door would open, or not open, or even push us away, it doesn't matter! the door would be there, and we would have to knock. But instead: we are obliged to knock without knowing where: this is what we need to understand. If I had chosen to struggle against someone, or against something, Marcel would be right. But I decided to struggle against evidences, that is against the all-powerfulness of impossibility.[10]

Le Lundi existentiel, with its title taken from a line in Kafka's diary,[11] was Fondane's philosophical last word, just as "Baudelaire" was

---

8. Russian writer and musicologist and Shestov's French translator.

9. Rachel Bespaloff, Russian philosopher, disciple of Shestov, and one of Heidegger's first commentators in French. Mary McCarthy's translation of her book *On the Iliad* has been reprinted in *War and the Iliad* (New York: New York Review of Books, 2005).

10. Fondane, "Sur les rives de l'Illissus," 86 (my translation).

11. "'You are reserved for a great Monday.' Fine, but Sunday will never end." From the November 2, 1921, entry in Franz Kafka, *Diaries, 1910–1923,* 397.

his final word in criticism. It was written for the volume *L'Existence* published by Gallimard in 1945 on the state of the art of existentialist thought, where the essay appears in second place following a piece by Albert Camus. The order is revealing. After Shestov's death in 1938 and Fondane's six years later, the second wave of existentialist thinkers, led by Camus and Jean-Paul Sartre, found an open field for their line of thought, taking over, as it were, the legacy of Kierkegaard and Nietzsche.

Yet Fondane always maintained that he had taken up philosophy to defend his poetry, that is, to articulate its dedication to lived experience in the face of mass culture and to the particular in the face of the general truths of the philosophers, notably the rationality of Kant and the idealism of Hegel. In a world where even the standard-bearers of revolt (read: the surrealists) advocated a clinical reliance on automation and an art that was autonomous and divorced from life, he looked to poetry as the fundamentally existential and even heroic and subversive act that could reassert the individual's humanity and place in the world. So it would be wrong to read *Ulysses* as a philosophical poem in the sense that it expresses a philosophical doctrine or even a philosophical view. Rather, the writing of such a poem was itself the philosophical assertion par excellence, while the philosophy properly speaking that Fondane practiced was his attempt to argue why. This line of thought is most forcefully laid out in *Faux traité d'esthétique*. Poetry, "inasmuch as it refuses to be a form of knowledge," is the way to break through the wall of reason's imperatives and replace them with the only evidences that are truly universal: the existential truths of life, death, and individual experience.

Benjamin Fondane was naturalized a French citizen in 1938, and when war broke out in 1940 he was called to serve in the French army. After the French capitulation,[12] he spent time as a prisoner of

---

12. "and we were gathered up by the roads / with broken horses and mangled trucks" (XIII).

war (escaping, being recaptured) before being released on grounds of ill health. Victoria Ocampo arranged for him to come to Argentina, but the French government was no longer issuing exit visas, and his last years in occupied Paris were a time of both forced idleness and feverish activity. Refusing to wear the yellow star, he also refused to go into hiding. Fondane's writings from even his earliest years were already pervaded with a prophetic sense of portent and misfortune; now faced with the urgency of an existence with no future, and the overwhelming pressure of the events around him, he turned to what he had already accomplished—"to *Ulysses*, of course," he said in a letter to Fredi Guthmann.[13] He found himself dissatisfied with his poem that was already ten years old, and having "nothing else to do" (surely a disingenuous statement, if ever there was one), he set to revising it directly on the 1933 copy, crossing out and rewriting, cutting and pasting, adding whole new sections. A typewritten page was found stuck to one of the penultimate drafts[14] that puts into perspective much of what has been said above about the final version of the poem itself:

> This second version of Ulysses is taking form day by day (it isn't finished) by a man just barely returned from the prison camp and the hospital and whom the police are hunting at every crossroads. Perhaps it will be completed before he loses his freedom, perhaps it will be interrupted, like the too-famous poem of Chenier. These conditions seem like they should be extraneous to poetry in general—but they are not extraneous to this poem in particular.
>
> By a strange sort of irony, here the universal meets the particular, and action turns out to be no less than the sister of the dream. Naturally this wasn't the case, the agreement was far from perfect, when the poem was conceived around 1929. At the time, it

13. Monique Jutrin, "Du mal d'Ulysse au mal des fantômes," 121. First published by Louis Soler in *Cahiers Benjamin Fondane* 1.

14. Ms. 7072, Bibliothèque Jacques Doucet, quoted in ibid., along with the letter to Guthmann.

was a matter of a pure and timeless poetic material, a view of reality through the typical layers of distant experience. Unfortunately, current events were brutally imposed on these images—they give a color of immediacy to what had already become spirit and form, a color of hic et nunc [here and now] to what had existed sub specie aeterni [under the aspect of eternity].

The naive reader might believe that the poet drew his poetry directly from imminent experience—as if that were possible. But it is true that a current trauma—which by its very essence is destructive of the creative affectivity—can reveal a trauma that is already old, already healed, but analogous—and cause the poetry to break through to another, further, level. This explains why, being unable to set ourselves to writing anything new, we have returned to Ulysses. And perhaps there was also the anxiety of perfection, in the midst of precariousness and instability.[15]

In 1942, while he was still at work on successive versions of *Ulysses*, Fondane began writing the "masterpiece of his 40th year," *The Sorrow of Ghosts*.[16] In this highly formal long poem, the themes of Ulysses undergo a poetic transmutation and emerge as a refined culmination of his previous work. The ghosts who wait on the quay to embark, fleeing a world falling to pieces, crossing the ocean in giant steamers, share much with the voyager Ulysses, traveling incessantly onward, searching back in his own past, never arriving. They are both fatally estranged, from that lost world that was never theirs in the first place, from their own past (like Fondane himself, who never seemed quite sure how to confront his own Jewish heritage), and, as seekers of a hard truth like Shestov, from the crowds around them who accepted the world as they saw it.

Benjamin Fondane and his beloved sister, Line, were arrested by the French police on March 7, 1944, and sent to the internment camp at Drancy. Fondane's influential friends managed to secure his release

---

15. Jutrin, "Du mal d'Ulysse," 120.
16. See my translation in *Cinepoems and Others*.

on the grounds of his "Aryan" marriage, but he refused to leave his sister, and both were sent to Auschwitz at the end of May. The last report of Fondane comes from a fellow detainee. Lazar Moscovici was a Romanian doctor who knew the poet from his Romanian writings; in a 1981 interview he recounts how he and others maneuvered to keep Fondane from being sent to the gas chambers when his health began to fail and recalls the surprising intimacy of their last weeks:

> I still remember those harrowing evenings when he would recite for us fragments of his poem *Ulysses*, begun in Paris, and which was intended as an elegy for the Jewish people and a symbol of his own fate. With what tenderness did he speak of his wife Geneviève, of his "own place" in Paris, of his books, his paintings, his fine Romanian carpets, of that setting we could imagine, that atmosphere of warmth and friendship, brotherhood and humanity.
>
> It could not last. The Moloch was calling for victims.[17]

If the poetry of Benjamin Fondane seems strange to us, it may be because beyond so many individual lives, it was a world that went up in smoke at Auschwitz, a world in which philosophy mattered, in which the struggles and contradictions of daily existence could be conceived in philosophical terms. Nothing could be further from the concrete, scientific spirit that characterizes both life and literature in America today. Yet inasmuch as Fondane's philosophy was ultimately a *lived* philosophy, and his poetry a visceral expression of individual existence, the words still speak to us. Despite, and indeed because of, the change of context, their urgency has not abated.

17. Excerpted from an interview with Moscovici in *Dialogue*, no. 7 (1981). Quoted in *Benjamin Fondane: Roumanie, Paris, Auschwitz*, 117.

A Note on the Text

The French text is based on the 2006 Verdier edition, established by Patrice Beray and Michel Carassou with the collaboration of Monique Jutrin. A few further corrections provided by Agnès Lhermitte and Professor Jutrin from the manuscript in the Bibliothèque Doucet have been taken into account.

Ulysses

à Armand Pascal,
dans la mort . . .

Et c'est l'heure, ô Poète,
de décliner ton nom,
ta naissance et ta race
　　　　—SAINT-JOHN PERSE, *Exil*

No retreat, no retreat
They must conquer or die
who have no retreat
　　　　—Mr. Gay

for Armand Pascal,
in death . . .

And this is the hour, O Poet,
to state your name,
your race and your descent
       —SAINT-JOHN PERSE, *Exile*

No retreat, no retreat
They must conquer or die
who have no retreat
       —Mr. Gay

J'étais un grand poète né pour chanter la Joie
—mais je sanglote dans ma cabine,
des bouquets d'eau de mer se fanent dans les vases
l'automne de mon cœur mène au Père-Lachaise,
l'éternité est là, œil calme du temps mort
est-ce arriver vraiment que d'arriver au port?
Armand ta cendre pèse si lourd dans ma valise.

Voici ta vie immense qui fait sauter les ponts.
Tu sais nager, je sais, mais que le fleuve est long!
Nous étions écrasés par cette lumière inhumaine.
Pourquoi chanter à tue-tête? Gorge pleine
qui ne demande qu'à chanter?
Si le château était hanté?
si les dieux s'amusaient à nous prendre pour cible?
Tu es entré vivant aux mains du dieu terrible
et jusque dans la mort tu es resté vivant . . .
. . . Que le flot ne veut-il m'emporter?
                                             Océan
ta vague furieuse fouette le vieil automne!

À l'hôpital cette blancheur d'angoisse, jaune.
Que de bateaux ici chassés par les typhons,
blessés dans leur ferraille tendre
ont coulé par le fond!
Des visiteurs parfois y entrent en scaphandres
qui gardent en esprit la corde qui les lie
au monde extérieur. Ils pensent à ce monde
tout le temps qu'ils sont là, penchés sur quelque lit,
et les mourants y pensent aussi et des bulles d'air montent
à la surface. Mais que font donc les vivants?
qu'attendent-ils pour mettre en marche les poulies?
Le film, le film est-il tellement captivant
que projette la mort sur l'écran de la vie?

I was a great poet, born to sing Joy
—but I am sobbing in my berth,
bouquets of seawater wilt in the vase
the autumn of my heart leads to Père-Lachaise,
eternity is there, calm eye of a dead time
is this the last call, coming at last to port?
Armand, your ashes are so heavy in my suitcase.

Here is your vast life, that blew the bridges to the sky.
You know how to swim, I know, but the river is long!
We were crushed by this inhuman light.
Why sing at the top of our lungs? Wide throat
that only asks to sing?
What if the castle was haunted?
if the gods passed their time by taking shots at us?
Alive, you entered the hands of the terrible god
and even in death remained alive . . .
. . . Why will the river's waters not bear me off? ∕·
                                  Ocean
your furious waves lash the faded autumn.

At the hospital, the whiteness of dread, and yellow.
So many boats here, driven by some typhoon
their tender scrap iron battered,
have sunk to the bottom.
Visitors sometimes come in diving suits,
they hold in their hearts the cord that ties them
to the world outside: they think of that world
the whole time they are here, bent over a bed
and the dying think of it too and bubbles rise
to the surface. But what are the living up to,
what are they waiting for to start the pulleys?
Is it so captivating, the film, the film
that death projects on the screen of life?

Oh que ta voix est lasse
laisse-moi près de ta voix
splendide, tu jouais avec le ciel d'en face
je veux dormir près de tes mains
le grand rideau tombait avant la fin et cependant
la vie applaudissait de se sentir émue
dans les cris d'autobus, les accidents, les bris,
elle applaudissait à tout rompre
—pourquoi ne pas venir saluer le public?
Une aube d'au-delà sur ton visage tremble /. .

Ami, ami nous étions venus de loin, ensemble,
unis comme les branches des ciseaux
pépins d'un même fruit
le même rêve à partager, le même pain
la même soif plus grande que le monde.
Nous avions de quoi conquérir plus qu'un monde:
Nous aura-t-on trompés, rusés?
Sisyphe, vieux Sisyphe que tu es donc usé!
Céderas-tu? consentirais-je
au seul droit de la force?
Ce n'était rien, un piège.
Il ne faut pas céder. Pas d'issue, pas d'issue!
Ils doivent périr ou vaincre ceux qui n'ont point d'issue! /

Quelle barque jamais, au royaume des cieux,
aborda sans péril, par calme plat? Tes yeux
se sont peut-être ouverts ailleurs. Mais la tempête
ce soir t'a rejeté sur nos bords. Salut, mouette!
Entends-tu l'océan pendant que tu es là?
Tu es au moins aussi vivant que moi,
tu es mon rire et ma mémoire
je suis enceint de ta mort
je te porte plus haut que mon buste,
je hais la mort, je hais la vie.
J'ai si grand pitié des hommes)

6   BENJAMIN FONDANE

Oh how your voice is weak
let me stay near your voice
magnificent, you played with the facing sky
I want to sleep near your hands
the great curtain fell before the end and yet
life applauded, deeply moved
in the cries of buses, accidents, broken glass
it clapped as hard as it could
—why not come out and greet the public?
A dawn of hereafter trembles in your face . . .

My friend, my friend, we came from far away, united
like a pair of scissor blades,
seeds of the same fruit,
sharing the same dream, the same bread
the same thirst greater than the world.
We had what it took to conquer more than one world:
could we have been deceived, taken in?
Sisyphus, old Sisyphus, you are so worn out!
Will you give in? Will I concede
to the rule of force?
It was nothing, a trap.
We must not give in. No retreat, no retreat!
They must die or conquer, who have no retreat!

What ship will ever, in the kingdom of heaven,
make land without danger, the sea flat and calm? Your eyes
have opened elsewhere, perhaps. But the storm
this evening flung you on our shore. Greetings, gull!
Do you hear the ocean from where you are?
You are at least as alive as I,
you are my laughter, my memory,
I am pregnant with your death
I carry you higher than my chest
I hate death, I hate life.
I feel such pity for men

je me hais et je m'aime
pardonne-moi d'être vivant, d'écrire des poèmes,
je suis encore là mais je parle aux fantômes!
Est-il réponse ou non aux questions de l'homme
quelque part? Et le dieu existe-t-il, le Dieu
d'Isaïe, qui essuiera toute larme des yeux
et qui vaincra la mort—
quand les premières choses seront évanouies?

I hate myself, and I love myself
forgive me for being alive, for writing poems
I am still here but I speak to ghosts!
Is there an answer somewhere to the questions
of men? And does god exist, the God
of Isaiah, who will wipe every tear from the eye,
and who will overcome death—
when the first things have passed?

Cette nuit une lampe oubliée, allumée,
vacilla tout à coup en moi comme un oiseau
l'aile meurtrie et déplumée . . .
Était-ce bien le *même* monde?
était-ce un monde renversé?
. . . Elle était là encore la Terre, elle était ferme,
et pourtant j'entendais ses craquements futurs
—il ne faut pas s'y attarder
—il ne faut pas lui faire confiance,
quelque chose aura lieu. Quelque chose, mais Quoi?

Les événements couraient les uns après les autres
ils se suivaient au galop,
leur chevelure était fuyante
—à quoi bon regarder en avant, en arrière?
ce fleuve allait, bien sûr, m'emporter dans ses eaux,
la vie allait, bien sûr, me traverser de part en part
—je vous salue, ô richesses!
que ferais-je à présent de tous ces rubans de lumière,
de ces choses qui naissent de l'eau, du crépuscule,
j'errais aveugle dans le pas perdu des gares
je demandais aux trains le but de mon voyage
pourquoi voulais-je aller si loin, quitter mon lit,
nourrir ma fièvre de banquises?
Juif, naturellement, tu étais juif, Ulysse,
tu avais beau presser l'orange, l'univers,
le sommeil était là, assis, les yeux ouverts,
l'espace était immangeable,
le sang mordait au vide et se sentait poreux
un gros poisson touchait au monde, de sa queue
—son cri était long et sordide . . .

. . . la fin du monde et moi, ici, sur le balcon?
J'appelais au secours, d'une voix d'exception

Last night a forgotten lamp
flickered inside me, suddenly like a bird
with a battered and plucked wing . . .
Was it really the *same* world?
was it a world inverted?
. . . The Earth was still there, still solid
and yet I heard the sound of its future breaking
—we must not linger here
—we must not trust in it,
something will happen. Something, but What?

Events came running one after another
they followed each other at a gallop
their hair thrown back
—what good is looking ahead or back?
this river was always going to bear me off
and life was always going to go right through me
—hail, O riches!
what would I have done with all those ribbons of light?
with those things that are born of water, of twilight,
I wandered blindly through the endless halls of stations
I asked the trains what was the end of my voyage
why did I want to go so far, to leave my bed
and stoke my fervor for seas of ice?
A Jew, naturally you were a Jew, Ulysses,
for all you squeezed the orange, the universe,
sleep was there, seated, its eyes open wide
space was inedible
your blood bit into the void and felt washed-through
a huge fish touched the world with its tail
—and gave a long and sordid cry . . .

. . . the end of the world, and me, here on the balcony?
I called for help with a voice of exception

mais à quoi bon me plaindre, geindre?
Un bonheur inconnu me léchait les reins,
je criais d'être libre, heureux, mais l'épouvante
me jetait un soleil cruel, à peine mûr,
il pourrissait au contact de mes mains
—qu'en ferais-je?

Seul! J'étais seul au monde avec moi-même,
feuille morte pareille à une feuille morte.

but what is the use of groaning, complaining?
An unknown pleasure licked the small of my back
I cried to be free and happy, but fear
threw me a cruel sun, barely ripe,
that rotted as soon as it touched my hands
—what could I do with that?

Alone, I was alone in the world with myself,
dead leaf resembling any dead leaf.

Préface

Il y avait longtemps
que le spectacle était commencé de l'Histoire
on en avait déjà oublié les débuts
les origines fabuleuses,
quand je suis né au monde
au milieu de l'Intrigue
comme un événement prévu depuis toujours
et cependant comme une surprise
un personnage inquiétant
qui pouvait tout laisser en place, qui pouvait tout changer,
le sens de l'action, la trame des mobiles,
qui avait sur le texte établi de toujours
l'ascendant prodigieux, étrange du vivant
le droit de bafouiller les meilleures répliques
d'improviser un monde en marge de l'Auteur
et tout à coup, malgré le Plan,
s'introduire soi-même au sein du personnage
en criant, excédé, vers le public des loges
«Il n'y a pas assez de réel pour ma soif!»

Preface

The performance
of History had already begun,
the beginning, the fabulous origins
were long forgotten
when I awoke to the world
in the thick of the Intrigue
like an event foretold since the beginning
and yet a surprise
a troubling character who could
leave everything untouched, who could change it all
the line of action, the weave of motives,
who had over the long established text
the strange prodigious force of the living
the right to stumble over the best lines
to improvise a world in the margins of the Author
and suddenly, despite the Plan,
to slip himself into the character
shouting furiously to the public in their boxes
"There is not enough *real* for my thirst!"

I

Variante

Le monde s'ouvre en nous par la vue des navires
qui partent—comme ils partent leur chevelure au vent
qui rentrent—comme ils rentrent, vieillis et décrépits,
dans le bal des lumières,
dans la fête d'adieu des ports,
pareils à des infirmes
assis, pendant qu'on danse!

Le monde s'ouvre en nous par des matins immenses
(en ai-je vu briller aux cils de l'océan!)
par des fées enfermées
dans le noyau des fruits où les enfants ont peur,
par des tapis jetés sous les pieds de la Reine
(comme elle avance calme dans le pays des palmes)
par des chansons de nègres sur le Mississippi
(ont-ils été aussi chassés du Paradis?)
et tout à coup par des pays de cheminées,
des asiles de nuit
où s'écoulent les eaux verdâtres de l'humain
en ai-je vu? et par des tripots clandestins,
des Parques de l'ennui
qui tricotent des bas de laine pour les morts.

Le monde s'ouvre en nous (où en es-tu ma Soif?)
par un mélange huileux de races et de langues,
par le murmure long et doux des épitaphes
(où? quand? dans quelles landes?)
—par des marins de sable qui demandent du sable,
perdus dans le sable, cherchant un monde à oublier
—par le vomissement sans fin de l'incurable
criant pour s'entendre crier
(oh! les nuits et leur peine!)
—par les danseuses ivres des jours et des semaines.

16   BENJAMIN FONDANE

I
Variant

The world unfolds within us at the sight of ships
departing—as they depart with their hair in the wind
returning—as they return old and decrepit
in the dance of lights,
in the farewell revels of ports,
like invalids
seated, while everyone else is dancing.

The world unfolds within us at vast mornings
(what ones I saw, glistening on the ocean's lashes!)
at fairies trapped
in fruit pits where children are afraid,
at carpets unrolled before the feet of the Queen
(advancing calmly in the land of palms)
at songs of blacks on the Mississippi
(were they, too, chased from Paradise?)
and suddenly at miles of chimneys,
of night shelters
where the greenish bilge of humanity runs out
(I've seen my share) and at clandestine gambling dens,
the Fates of weary lives
knitting wool stockings for the dead.

The world unfolds within us (how have you fared, my Thirst?)
at an oily mix of languages and race
at the long and gentle murmur of epitaphs
(where? and when? and on what coastal plains?)
—by sailors of sand who ask for sand
lost in the sand, seeking a world to forget
—at the endless vomiting of the incurable
crying out to hear itself cry
(oh! the nights and their pain!)
—at the dancers drunk for days and weeks on end.

—N'avons-nous pas assez navigué dans la poisse,
sans demander quartier, sans implorer merci?
Il est temps de fermer les portes, temps d'éteindre
la lampe. Il est grand temps
de signer cette fresque qu'on a fini de peindre
—et qu'emporte le vent.

—Have we not drifted long enough through the fog
without asking quarter or begging mercy?
It is time to close the doors, time to switch off
the lamp. At last it is time
to sign this fresco we have painted
—and that the wind sweeps away.

J'ai quitté les trottoirs de la ville pour d'autres trottoirs de villes,
les millions d'hommes pour d'autres millions d'hommes,
les mêmes à n'en plus finir,
je n'en avais jamais assez!
Pourquoi me suis-je déplacé?
Les mots se meurent de changer de bouche,
la chance s'use de fournir les dés.
Quel curieux voyage j'ai fait parmi les hommes,
que de routes avons-nous parcourues ô mon œil
et quel étonnement à chaque tournant neuf
que les matins fussent les mêmes,
que les hommes eussent même visage,
vieux canots amarrés aux pontons pourrissants,
existences jaunies—
ne savais-je donc pas leur racine enfouie
sous terre—et le voyage inutile, et la soif?
C'est dans leur tubercule qu'il y avait du neuf!
Miracles de la faim, du froid,
vous êtes si plein de figures! ⟩

— Que le monde était plein quand nous avons quitté
le port! Était-ce une vue ou bien une vision?
Et maintenant que les mers ont salé mes poumons
mouette vieillie, espoir usé et ébruité
je ferme le vieux livre et je dis: À quoi bon?
Pourquoi tant d'eau multipliée par tant d'eau,
tant de terre?
L'Homme est peut-être roi de ce monde, mais moi
mais vous, toutes ces ombres usées par la colère,
la pitié et l'envie de n'être nulle part,
qu'y cherchons-nous? Vous ai-je inventées? Mon regard
est las. Que font les hommes? Sont-ils absents d'eux-mêmes?—
Ou bien, rongés de fièvres secrètes comme nous,
revenus d'un voyage où eux aussi avaient

II

I left one city's sidewalks for other city sidewalks,
millions of men for other millions of men,
the same ones, on and on without end,
I never had enough!
So why had I gone?
Words fade from passing from mouth to mouth
and luck wears out from furnishing the dice.
What a curious voyage I have made among men,
how many roads have we traveled, O my eye,
and what amazement at each new turn
to find that the mornings were the same,
that men had the same faces,
old dinghies tied to rotting wharves,
yellowed existences—
did I not know their root was buried
deep in the earth—and the voyage useless, and the thirst?
The novelty was in their tubercles!
Miracles of hunger, of cold,
you are so full of faces!

The world seemed so full as we were leaving
port! Was it a vision, or did we see true?
And now that the seas have salted my lungs
timeworn seagull, hope chipped and worn
I close the old book and ask: What use?
Why so much water multiplied by so much water,
and so much land?
Man may be king of this world, but I
but you, all these shadows worn down by anger,
pity, and desire to be nowhere at all,
what are we seeking? Did I invent you? My gaze
is tired. What are men up to, are they absent from themselves?—
or rather consumed, like us, by secret fevers,
returned from voyages where they too

vu des êtres, des ports et des mers insensées,
des choses éternelles, si fades au palais,
et de sensibles, tendres et périssables choses
—si chères!
/

saw people, ports and absurd seas,
eternal things, that are so dull to the palate,
and feeling, tender, perishable things
—so dear!

III

Je ne saurais vous dire l'eau.

Je me sens précédé, je me sens suivi d'elle,
elle fouette le cœur
elle m'écrase l'œil et calomnie les distances
elle est malpropre et crache le destin
du pouce elle façonne le temps
elle exige des volontaires.

Je viens d'une petite ville blanche où pissaient les vaches
les soleils débordaient le soutien-gorge des haies,
une odeur de matin qui s'est lavée à l'eau
des fourmis longuement marchaient sur les mains calmes
une chèvre broutait du lait
laitues fraîches vous vous êtes tues,
la chair était si calme—
ville de petits juifs accrochés à l'air
les trottoirs étaient des rubans sales,
j'étouffais de bonheur, de dégoût,
ça sentait le pain frais et le hareng salé
l'amour sentait la bouse humide . . .
. . . j'ai chanté tout cela, mais je voulais partir
je voulais l'univers désertique,
je voulais les villes énormes où le soleil est noir
déchirer la chemise des hommes
leur crier ma démence et ma soif . . .
Je voulais l'Océan infertile, salé, souple.
—Océan! Je te serre sur ma poitrine!
Tu es beaucoup trop grand, mais tes cheveux sont fins,
dans ma petite ville je te croyais si fort,
ta puissance comblait mes reins . . .
Devais-je un jour te rencontrer si pâle?
À la criée des poissons je t'ai senti tout nu

III

for Geneviève

I cannot tell you about water.

I feel that it precedes me, I feel it follows me,
it lashes my heart
it crushes my eyes and slanders distances
it is unclean and spits out destiny
it models time with its thumb
it demands volunteers.

I come from a small white town of pissing cows
where suns overflowed the corseted hedges,
a smell of water-washed mornings
of ants walking a long time over calm hands,
a goat grazed milk
fresh lettuce, you've fallen quiet
the flesh was so calm—
town of small Jews suspended in the air
the sidewalks were dirty ribbons
I choked with happiness, with disgust,
the place smelled of salt herring and fresh bread
love smelled of moist manure . . .
. . . I sang all that, but wanted to leave,
I wanted the barren universe,
I wanted great cities where the sun shines black,
to tear men's shirts, to shout
at them my madness and my thirst . . .
I wanted the salty, supple, infertile Ocean.
—Ocean, I clasp you to my breast.
You're much too large, but your hair is so fine . . .
in my little town I believed you were so strong
your force fulfilled my desires . . .
Did I need to find you at last, so pale?
At the fishmongers' cries I felt you so exposed

—souffres-tu comme les hommes?
Tes yeux me font pitié, tes yeux brûlés,
si tu pouvais au moins t'arrêter un instant
—ta marche est inlassable!
Quelle terrible solitude, dis?
Si je pouvais je t'aimerais comme une sœur
je t'aiderais à traverser les zones inhumaines
—la main dans la main.

—do you suffer like men?
Your eyes fill me with pity, your burned-out eyes,
if only you could rest for a moment
—your tread is unrelenting!
What terrible solitude, no?
If I could, I would love you as a sister
I would help you cross these inhuman zones
—hand in hand.

IV

Pourquoi l'océan me fait-il penser à ces plaines de Bessarabie,
on y marchait longtemps et c'était long la vie.
Steppe! ce fond de mer agaçait les narines
l'œil de la terre s'ouvrait sous les paupières marines
on avançait sans avancer et on faisait le point.
Notre marche avançait la distance d'autant.

—Parfois un paysan égaré cherchait les racines des eaux . . .
eaux longuement sollicitées,
terres longtemps voulues,
le regard sommeillait de ne heurter rien,
l'espace de lui-même a engendré l'espace,
le temps gonflé et dégonflé,
la nuit, le jour, la même mer tranquille, lisse—
a-t-on bientôt touché aux côtes d'Amérique?
Dites-moi, Commandant, était-il VRAI le port d'attache,
allons-nous voir les paysans meugler comme des vaches—
—cette mer, cette terre, rien ne les presse de finir?

—J'ai vu ces paysans en 1914
fuir les Autrichiens, quitter la terre au cou des bœufs,
de leurs corps ils ensemençaient la terre vieille
ils fuyaient la mort pour la mort,
la guerre était si longue, le naufrage infini,
que les hommes soudain envahissaient les routes
ivres d'on ne sait quel espace qui coulait
autour du cou, comme une corde, et qui tirait.
Cela sombrait à vue d'œil,
ils lâchaient les maisons qui sentaient l'incendie,
le petit pré si doux aux naseaux du cheval,
le puits comme une bouche dont la langue est fraîche,
le bel oignon juteux, la betterave rêche,
la toute petite église en bois où les aïeux
savaient un escalier qui les menait aux cieux.

IV

Why does the ocean bring to mind those Bessarabian plains,
we walked there a long time and life was long.
Steppe! that seafloor stung the nose
the eye of the earth looked out through eyelids of sea
we advanced without advancing and took our bearings.
Walking, our step advanced as far.

—A peasant, lost, might go in search of the water's roots . . .
waters long implored,
lands long awaited,
our eyes, encountering nothing, grew heavy
space engendered from itself space
time swelled and sank back,
night, day and always the smooth and tranquil sea—
soon did we reach the coasts of America?
Tell me, Captain, was it REAL, the home port,
will we see the peasants bellowing like cows—
—this sea, this land, does nothing press them to come to an end?

—I saw those peasants in 1914
fleeing the Austrians, leading their oxen, leaving the land,
they sowed the old earth with their bodies
they were fleeing death for death,
the war went on so long, the shipwreck infinite,
that suddenly men thronged the roads
drunk on some expanse that slipped
around their necks like a rope, and pulled.
Everything sinking as they looked on,
they left their houses that smelled of fire,
the little field so sweet to the horse's nostrils,
the well like a mouth whose tongue is fresh and cool,
the fine juicy onion, the rough beet
the small wooden church where their ancestors
knew a stairway that led to Heaven

. . . Notre-Dame des Blés, du Maïs, et de l'Orge,
Toi qui sais que les cales du monde prennent l'eau,
Aie pitié de ces hommes de 1914—
aie pitié de ces rats qui fuient le bateau.

. . . Our Lady of Corn, of Barley, of Wheat,
You who know that the world is taking on water,
Have pity on these men of 1914—
have pity on these rats who flee the boat.

V

J'entre dans le mouvement qui me fuit, et j'ai peur,
mes mains, mes mains et ce qu'elles tiennent du monde.
Dans le passé sanglote une bouche ouverte,
ce n'est qu'une chanson pour le pays des ombres
    les travaux sont finis
    bus les paysages,
    à quoi bon repartir
    pour d'anciens voyages,
j'ai beau me déchirer pour aller de l'avant, rompre le poids de l'inertie!
Bagnard, le mouvement perpétuel t'attend, pèse aux parois de la
    vessie
—quelles mers vais-je encore teindre de mes désirs?
quelles terres brosser de songe?
Allez, allez la route!
Garçon! un peu plus d'atlantique!
La côte s'use, s'use
la vitrine un instant brûle sa féerie
—puis meurt.//
Désormais la face de Dieu seule où la nuit crache longuement,
et s'essouffle et reprend d'une salive nouvelle.
Et, que cela ne mène qu'aux terres inhumaines,
qu'aux ports désaccordés comme de vieux pianos
et qu'il faille carder, sur des métiers nouveaux
la trame usée du même . . .
Qu'il ferait bon téter ton lait sauvage, ô vie,
que des clous seraient bons pour raviver le sang
qu'une tempête serait bienvenue, violente,
une tempête, une émeute.
J'ai soif de toi, échevelée,
pendant que mon œil fuit
le blanc vol de mouettes
douces comme un sanglot irréel de la chair.

V

I join the fleeing movement and am afraid,
my hands, my hands and what they hold of the world.
An open mouth is sobbing in the past,
but it is only a song for the land of shadows
    our work is done
    the landscapes drained
    why set out again
    on old voyages
for all I strain to go ahead, to break the weight of inertia!
Convict, perpetual motion awaits you, it presses the walls of your
    bladder
—what seas have I yet to stain with my desires?
what lands paint with dreams?
Onward, onward the road!
Waiter! a little more Atlantic, please!
The coast wears down, wears away
for an instant the window flares its masque
—then dies.
Now only the face of God, where night relentlessly spits
then pauses breathless then starts again with fresh saliva.
And that this only leads to inhuman lands,
to ports as out of tune as old pianos
that we must card, on new looms,
the worn thread of the same . . .
How good it would be to suck your wild milk, O life,
and nails so good to revive the sleeping blood,
a storm's violence would be so welcome,
a storm, a riot.
I thirst for you, disheveled,
while my eye flees
the white flight of the gulls
soft like an unreal sob of the flesh.

Cri de la chair, esprit, vieil instrument de rêve!
Je ne peux te quitter! je ne peux te garder!
Je me penche anxieux sur le vieux bois—il chante.
Chantes-tu? souffres-tu?
Te voici les mamelles pleines de sève éparse
Est-ce appétit de croissance?
—soif d'inconnu vorace?
—te dresses-tu contre la mort
—est-ce la mort qui baise tes lèvres incertaines?

À présent, oubliée,
tu t'oublies toi-même.
Que t'importe le monde,
en es-tu donc sortie?

Une ombre t'a frôlée et s'est évanouie.
Tu souffres. Tu te couches

à bord du *Mendoza*, le 30/VII/29.

Cry of the flesh, spirit, old instrument of dreams!
I cannot leave you, cannot keep you!
Anxious, I lean close to the old wood—it sings.
Do you sing? do you suffer?
See how your breasts are filled with thin sap
Is this appetite for growth?
—voracious thirst for the unknown?
—do you defy death
—is it death that kisses your hesitating lips?

For now, forgotten
you forget yourself.
What do you care for the world,
have you left it behind?

A shadow brushed against you and disappeared.
You suffer. You go to bed

aboard the *Mendoza*, 30/VII/29.

VI

Un enfant est né
une femme est morte.
Comme tu sanglotes
méditerranée!

La mère a crié
le père a prié
le Temps est passé
à côté de l'heure.

De l'éternité
un enfant est né.

Quelle saison calme
dans l'esprit vaincu! . . .
Que suis-je, qu'es-tu
au bord d'une larme?

VI

A child is born
a woman dies.
Mediterranean
how you sob!

The mother screamed
the father prayed
and Time slipped by
the hour at hand.

From eternity
a child is born.

What calm season
in the broken spirit! . . .
Who am I, or you
at the edge of a tear?

VII

J'ai fait escale dans les villes
avec des compagnons dont j'ignorais le nom
j'allais au-devant des visages
le regard, du dedans, émerveillait la chair,
—chair, cette ville était de chair, de cuir,
elle était mise en mouvement par des courroies vivantes
de transmission, elle lavait ses vieilles cathédrales,
les vieux pavés, le temps comme le linge sale
—elle criait sa gloire:
j'ai craché sur de l'Histoire:
J'ai eu faim à Séville d'une Espagnole véritable,
maigre comme un repas du Mercredi des Cendres,
elle vendait des canaris.
À Cadix, j'ai rêvé aux aubes de Paris.
J'ai maudit, à Dakar, les patries blanches,
j'ai appelé à moi le sable, le sommeil,
mon cœur était faible et si lâche:
—Almería, tu sentais l'ail . . .
Partout des gens assis dans des cafés, les banques.
Nous parlions aussi peu que possible leur langue,
nous visitions les vieilles églises où Jésus-Christ
peint et cloué au mur jette son cri!
Les temps de la prière étaient déjà passés,
vieux le cri, vieille la beauté,
il n'y avait que le sang de vivant, il coulait noir
des chevaux éventrés et dans les abattoirs,
une sourde émotion se formait dans la bouche:
«Entrez, Messieurs, voici les merveilles louches»
qu'étais-je venu faire dans ces forêts peuplées?
J'avais cherché un peu de silence en espèces,
un peu de soleil moins fatigué qu'une neige,
la femme au ventre plein traversait mon sang,
la vie, la vie allait éclater de plus belle

VII

I went ashore in towns
with companions though I did not know their names
I went out to meet the faces
the gaze, from within, infused the flesh with wonder
—flesh, that city was made of flesh, of hide,
it was set in motion by living transmission
belts, it washed its old cathedrals,
its old cobbles, and time like dirty laundry
—it shouted its glory:
I spit on History:
I hungered in Seville for a true Spaniard,
lean like an Ash Wednesday meal,
she was selling canaries.
In Cádiz I dreamed of Paris dawns.
I cursed, in Dakar, the white nations
I called for sand, and sleep,
my heart was weak and so afraid:
—Almería, you smelled of garlic . . .
Everywhere, banks and people sitting in cafés,
we spoke as little as possible their language,
we visited old churches where Jesus Christ
painted and nailed to the wall utters his cry!
The time of prayer was already past,
the cry was old, even beauty had aged
there was only the blood of the living that flowed black
from gutted horses and in the slaughterhouses,
a heavy emotion formed in the mouth:
"This way, Gentlemen, to see sleazy wonders"
what had I come for in these peopled woods?
I had only sought a little silence in cash,
a little sun less tired than falling snow,
woman with her full womb crossed my blood,
and life was going to surge more beautiful

j'étais né à Jassy, que cherchais-je à Oran
(dans les vitrines des coiffeurs les femmes belles?)
mon voyage fini, mon passé aboli
où vais-je aller porter mes pas? sur quels rivages?
quels visages humains me viendront appeler?
quelles fatigues surhumaines?
Je ne peux écouter tant de voix à la fois.
Qui parle? que disais-je? qui, celui qui écoute?
—Assez, assez vous dis-je,
la masse de mon corps me pèse plus que Dieu,
je ne peux plus lutter contre vents et marées,
je ne peux plus marcher; les routes sont barrées
—assez!

I was born in Iaşi, what was I looking for in Oran
(in the windows of hair salons, beautiful women?)
my journey done, my past erased
where will I carry my steps, on what shores?
what human faces will come to call for me?
what superhuman exhaustion?
I cannot listen to so many voices at once.
Who is speaking? what was I saying? who, he who listens?
—Enough, enough I tell you,
the weight of my body burdens me more than God,
I can no longer fight against winds and tides,
I can no longer walk; the roads are blocked
—enough!

VIII

Plus loin, ou c'est trop tard,
la lumière saignait son jus inimitable,
tristesse à table d'hôte aux ports balbutiants,
le phare nous précède,
la nuit rentre dans l'œil comme l'oiseau au nid,
qu'il fait tard, qu'il fait tard,
les émigrants ne cessent d'escalader la nuit
ils grimpent dans la nuit jusqu'à la fin du monde,
ils rompent comme frères leur lait et le partagent
un sanglot fait le tour du monde,
et nous irons, bris d'une vieille danse,
sur toute la terre, et plus loin,
porteurs d'un grand secret dont s'est perdu le sens,
crier au visage des hommes notre soif incurable . . .
—À quoi servirait notre vie,
à quoi nos batailles perdues,
sinon à un Triomphe dont s'est perdu le sens,
et pour porter en fraude aux hommes
sous l'œil absent des douaniers—
une nouvelle beauté panique.

VIII

Onward, or it will be too late,
the light was oozing its matchless blood,
sadness at common tables in stammering ports,
the lighthouse goes ahead of us,
night enters the eye as a bird its nest,
it's so late, it's so late,
the emigrants endlessly scale the heights of the night
they climb in the night until the end of the world
they break their milk like brothers and share it
a sob goes round the world
and we will go, shards of an old dance,
throughout the earth and further,
bearing a great secret whose meaning is lost,
to shout in the face of men our incurable thirst . . .
—What would have been the point of our lives,
or of our lost battles,
if not a Triumph whose meaning is lost,
and to smuggle across to men
under the customs agents' absent eye—
a new *panic* beauty.

IX

à Line

Marseille, tu chargeas les cales du bateau
d'émigrants qui montaient sous l'œil de la police,
ils sentaient la fatigue, l'ail,
ils étaient loqueteux et bredouilles.

—Où allez-vous mes frères?
Maquignons, rebouteux, marchands de vins, forains,
fripiers, diamantaires,
votre sang fouette mon sang, votre paupière me soulève,
vous chevauchiez la nuit des temps
vous êtes ma soif permanente
je vous ai vus quittant les poches des provinces
traînant quelques vertèbres molles sous vos chemises
les pogroms de l'Ukraine vous ont chassés des villes
vous n'aviez que votre vie dans les valises
maigres vifs comme bois roulés par les torrents,
pourquoi aller toujours de la fin vers les
commencements,
pourquoi lisez-vous donc votre livre à rebours,
vous n'arrivez jamais et vous partez toujours
quel âcre paradis
roule dans votre bile,
où courez-vous, assis
sur le pont, immobiles,
ressemeleurs de mots, bijoutiers d'accidents,
dites-moi d'où vous vient ce fleuve d'énergie?
Dans vos mains je lisais une ligne de vie
longue et cent fois brisée.

Où donc t'avions-nous amarré
canot de secours, synagogue?
Partout dans le vent, la marée
monte, sanglot du Décalogue!

44   BENJAMIN FONDANE

IX

for Line

Marseille, you loaded the holds of the boat
with emigrants who boarded under the gaze of the police
they smelled of garlic, of exhaustion,
they came in tatters, empty-handed.

—Where are you going, my brothers?
Horse dealers, bone setters, wine merchants, country peddlers,
ragpickers, diamond cutters,
your blood lashes my blood, your eyelid lifts me up
you rode the night of time immemorial
you are my abiding thirst
I saw you leaving provincial backwaters
dragging a few limp vertebrae under your shirts
the Ukrainian pogroms drove you from the cities
you carried in your suitcase only your lives
lean lives like timber rolled by the rapids,
why always go from the end back to the
beginnings,
and your book, why do you read it backward,
you never arrive and are always leaving
what bitter paradise
flows in your bile,
where are you running, sitting
on deck, immobile,
resowers of words, jewelers of accidents,
tell me, where do you draw this river of energy?
I traced a lifeline in your hands that was
long and broken a hundred times.

Where did we make you fast,
lifeboat, synagogue?
Around us, the wind, the tide
rising, sob of the Decalogue!

Pauvres vifs
Que de fois projetés sur les murs par vos longues bougies de suif
vos ombres ont prié sur les fruits de la terre,
ont nagé lourdement dans l'eau de la prière
et appelé dans leurs cœurs racornis, la jeune,
la frêle bergère, l'épouse,
la fiancée promise et noire du Cantique
des Cantiques.

J'ai voyagé avec vous dans le train, mon père est là
(qu'il est beau dans ses yeux le maïs de la terre moldave).
Il est l'agent d'une Compagnie maritime du Havre,
il a la charge de ce convoi d'émigrants
il soigne ces galets de mer comme des diamants,
il gémit de temps en temps Ribono Schelolom!
En esprit il parle à Dieu, mais il pense au pogrom,
il pense à cette histoire (que de fois répétée)
d'exodes de vieillards fuyants avec leur thora,
     leurs édredons et les enfants à la tétée
que de fois faudra-t-il que la mer Rouge s'ouvre,
que nous criions vers toi du fond de notre gouffre,
la sortie de l'Égypte n'était-elle qu'une figure
de cette fuite éperdue le long de l'histoire future,
et Jérusalem n'était-il que symbole et que fable
de ce havre qu'on cherche et qui est introuvable?
Mon père, c'est cela qui te rend misérable.
Tu penses à ton jeune garçon que tu as emmené en voyage,
qui est si gentil en marin, mais si bête pour son âge,
il ne sait pas encore naviguer dans la mer des visages,
il a un monde en lui-même et rarement quitte le fond
pour respirer à la surface comme font les poissons,
il ne comprend rien à ce meeting de fantômes
que l'on roule d'un bout à l'autre du royaume
il a des yeux de marin, il est si fier de son rôle,
il trouve si jolies en photo les scènes de viol,

Poor wretches
Cast on the walls so many times by your long tallow candles
your shadows prayed over the fruit of the earth,
and swam laboriously in the waters of prayer
and called, in their stiffened hearts, for the young
delicate shepherdess, the betrothed,
the black and promised bride of the Song
of Songs.

I took the train with you, my father is there
(the corn of Moldova resplendent in his eyes).
He is the agent of a Shipping Firm from Le Havre,
he is responsible for these emigrants
he handles these sea pebbles as if they were diamonds,
he murmurs from time to time Ribono Schelolom!
In his mind he speaks to God, but he thinks of the pogrom,
he thinks of this tale (retold so many times)
of exodus of the aged fleeing with their Torah
      their goose-down quilts and infants at the breast
how many times must the Red Sea part,
must we cry to you from the depths of our abyss:
so did the flight from Egypt only prefigure
this desperate flight the length of future history,
so was Jerusalem only the symbol and fable
of the port we search for, that cannot be found?
My father, this is what torments you.
You think of your young son whom you brought along,
so nice in his sailor suit but so dumb for his age,
he hasn't learned yet how to navigate this sea of faces
he has a world inside him whose depths he rarely leaves
to breathe at the surface as the fishes do,
he cannot understand this meeting of ghosts
that are trundled across the kingdom
he has sailor eyes, he is so proud of his role,
he finds so pretty the photographs of scenes of rape

il bâille quand on chante le Cantique des Cantiques,
tu lui parais trop noire, bergère Sulamite.
—Sulamite, je t'ai vue. Tu gisais sur la terre russe
ouverte comme un jeune melon, parmi le bric-à-brac
d'un univers hagard jeté sur le marché aux puces!
Elle chante encore en moi ta chevelure rousse
—non, on n'a pas encore fusillé le Cosaque!
Une vieille couvrait de toile cette nature morte.

Sulamite, si jamais je t'oublie . . . C'est là que mon enfance est morte
sous les yeux de mon père. Oh! que j'avais sommeil.
Le Tsar avait permis que ces morts fussent mis en cercueil,
tandis que d'autres morts maigres comme une prière
debout, sur les débris fumants,
n'osaient pas, n'osaient plus sangloter vers leur Dieu.
Ils ne posaient pas de questions
les siècles n'avaient pas apporté de réponse
il fallait s'avancer dans le regard de Dieu
comme des mouches dans la toile de l'araignée
bêtes de sacrifices,
ô trop cruellement aimés, ô trop suavement haïs,
sans savoir si du moins la mort allait chanter,
si elle allait chanter merveilleuse à la fin,
à la fin de cette vie de taureau éventré
dans l'arène, sous les yeux d'un public délirant
et qui pèse et qui soupèse ton agonie
ô dentelle, ô démence!
Qu'importe si la vie avait ou non un sens!

. . . Émigrant, émigrant où vas-tu?
Attends, mais attends-moi je viens,
trente ans, qu'est-ce après tout que trente ans de retard,
je m'éloignais du train mais je partais quand même,
était-elle si loin la terre américaine?

he yawns when the Song of Songs is sung,
you seem too black to him, Shulamite, shepherdess.
—Shulamite, I saw you. You lay on the Russian ground
split open like a fresh melon among the junk
of a gaunt universe unloaded at the flea market!
Your red hair sings inside me still
—no, they still have not shot the Cossack!
An old woman hid that still life with a piece of canvas.

Shulamite, if ever I forget you . . . It was there my childhood died
before my father's eyes. Oh! I was so sleepy.
The Czar allowed the burial of those dead
while other dead, lean like a prayer
standing on the smoking rubble,
dared not, no longer dared, pour out their grief to their God.
They asked no questions
the centuries had brought no answers
they had to advance in the eyes of God
like flies in the spider's web
sacrificial beasts,
O too cruelly loved, too smoothly hated,
not knowing at least if death would sing,
would sing splendidly at the end,
at the end of this bull's life, gutted
in the arena, in the eyes of the jubilant public
that weighs and weighs up your agony
O lace, O madness!
Does it matter if life had meaning or not?

. . . Emigrant, emigrant, where are you going?
Wait for me, just wait I'm coming,
thirty years, what in the end is thirty years too late,
I moved away from the train but still I left,
was the land of America really so far?

Vous étiez une preuve que la terre était ronde.
À Itzkani voici un poste frontière dans le monde.
L'auberge, dans la nuit, une île de corail.
La valse viennoise ouvrait la vanne au songe
pour la première fois j'ai vu du poivre rouge . . .

—Mon père qu'as-tu fait de mon enfance?
qu'as-tu fait du petit marin au regard bleu?
J'étais heureux, heureux parmi ces malheureux,
le poivre rouge c'était si nouveau!
Plus tard j'ai vu Charlot et j'ai compris les émigrants,
plus tard, plus tard moi-même . . .
Émigrants, diamants de la terre, sel sauvage,
je suis de votre race,
j'emporte comme vous ma vie dans ma valise,
je mange comme vous le pain de mon angoisse,
je ne demande plus quel est le sens du monde,
je pose mon poing dur sur la table du monde,
je suis de ceux qui n'ont rien, qui veulent tout
—je ne saurai jamais me résigner.

You were a proof the earth was round.
Here in Iţcani a border crossing to the world.
The inn a coral island in the night.
Viennese waltzes opened the sluice of dreams
I saw red pepper for the first time . . .

—My father, what have you done with my childhood?
What have you done with the little blue-eyed sailor?
I was happy, happy among them with their misfortunes
red pepper was so new!
Later, when I saw Chaplin I understood those emigrants,
later, much later myself . . .
Emigrants, diamonds of the earth, wild salt,
I am of your race,
Like you I carry my life in my suitcase,
I eat like you the bread of my affliction,
I ask no more for the meaning of the world,
I pound my fist on the table of the world,
I am one of those who have nothing, who want everything
—I will never be resigned.

X
Chanson de l'émigrant

Amer, le goût de notre sort!
À quoi servent sanglots et plaintes?
Pour le pain dur d'un passeport
on a pris nos empreintes.

Mon père couché sous la terre
jusqu'à l'heure du Jugement,
pourquoi as-tu peur que je meure?
pourquoi ai-je peur du vivant?

Nous ne parlons aucune langue,
nous ne sommes d'aucun pays,
notre terre c'est ce qui tangue
notre havre c'est le roulis.

Marchand d'appétits, vieille rosse,
me voici assis sur un sac,
le ciel du côté de mon gosse
et moi du côté du ressac.

Parmi le cuir fin des oranges,
parmi des massacres d'oignons,
je touche, absurdes compagnons,
aux grandes patries étranges.

Comme tu fonds dans mon gosier
sanglot du tropique!
Ni prier ni crier
sur la grand-route maléfique.

De Kiev, d'Irkutzk, de Varsovie,
pour São Paulo, pour Lima . . .
Mon Dieu, quelle chienne de vie
traînée de climat en climat!

X
Emigrant's Song

The taste of our fate is bitter!
What use are sobs and complaints?
For the hard bread of a passport
they took our fingerprints.

My father asleep in the ground
till Judgment Day arrives
why do you fear my death?
and why do I fear life?

We are speakers of no language,
we call no country home,
our land is the pitching steerage,
our haven the rolling swell.

Merchant of appetites,
old bore, I sit on a sack,
the sky on the side of my boy
and I, of the ship's wake.

Surrounded by orange rinds
and massacres of onions
I'm hemmed in, absurd companions,
by all the great foreign nations.

Oh, how you melt in my throat,
sob of tropical zones!
I will not cry nor pray
along the evil highway.

From Irkutsk, Warsaw, Kiev,
To São Paulo, or to Lima . . .
My God, what a bitch of a life
dragging from climate to climate!

Et quelle amertume, ô délice,
que de glisser, l'esprit à jeun
—sans matière, comme un parfum—,
entre les doigts de la police!

Rameurs d'une vieille fiction,
(quand donc finira le périple?)
nous naviguons dans le multiple
pays de la malédiction.

Ô mère cruelle, Existence!
Quelle louve, pour ses petits,
eut plus d'ovaires dans la panse,
et moins de lait dedans ses pis?

Sur ce maigre bateau fantôme
qui est à lui-même son port,
quelle longue java que l'homme
sur l'accordéon de la mort.

Que vienne la fin de ce monde!
Puisse-t-elle fermer nos yeux . . .
Menez toutes seules la ronde
étoiles qui êtes aux cieux.

Sommes-nous nés sur une route
qui avance et ne finit pas
afin de casser notre croûte
entre la terre et l'au-delà?

Et sommes-nous partis de l'Olt,
du Dniepr et de Crimée
afin de te porter, Révolte,
jusqu'aux entrailles du Créé?

. . . Mon père, couché sous la terre
les yeux ouverts dans le tombeau,

And what a bitter pleasure
to slip, the spirit unfed
—immaterial like perfume—
through the hands of the police!

At the oars of an age-old fiction
(this voyage, when will it end?)
we navigate the manifold
country of our curse.

O you're a cruel mother, Existence!
What she-wolf had for her brood
more ovaries in her paunch
and in her teats less food?

Aboard this lean ghost ship
that is for itself a port
man's life is a long Java
on death's accordion.

Let the world come to an end!
And may it close our eyes . . .
Continue the dance alone,
stars that are in the skies.

So were we born on a road
that travels on and on
that we may break our bread
between earth and the great beyond?

And did we leave the Olt,
the Dnieper and Crimea
to carry you, Revolt,
to the entrails of Creation?

. . . My father, asleep in the ground,
eyes open in the grave,

sais-tu qu'on est mieux sous ta pierre?
—Ici, la terre est toute d'eau.

On a pris nos empreintes
sur toute la terre, et plus loin.
À quoi servent sanglots et plaintes?
La route marche et ne finit point.

do you know it's better under your stone?
—Here the earth is all water and wave.

They took our fingerprints
throughout the earth and farther.
What's the use of sobs and complaints?
The road goes on and on.

Je me suis arrêté dans les ports où les marchands ambulants
sollicitaient l'esprit d'avoir soif de CHOSES
ils remaillaient de la trame chantante de leurs tapis
la lumière tendue de l'Afrique!

Cette lumière sèche flottait comme une toile au vent,
elle n'avait rien d'humain,
et cependant je descendais avec un grand chapeau de paille
suivre cette chanson inhumaine . . .

Étrange, la chanson! Étrange, cette soif
d'une pulpe, en moi-même, qui n'eût rien de tendre . . .

Après-midi incertaines!
Que j'aimais me pencher sur vos eaux incréées
comme un pêcheur à la ligne
j'espérais des poissons inconnus, des merveilles légères,
des équilibres nouveaux,
alors que la lumière tournait autour de moi
elle entrait dans mes poches comme un lézard heureux
si calme et si poreuse
cherchait-elle un secret perdu de ma substance?
Nous avions l'air d'inconnus qui ont dansé à un bal,
qui se sont un instant appuyés l'un sur l'autre
et qui ont craint de mêler leur sueur et leur songe,
alors qu'en eux se donnaient des festins fabuleux
des vins sans lendemain tintaient dans leurs oreilles,
et qu'une musique montait comme un jardin suspendu
—qui a tissé, savant, la toile d'araignée?
Nous avions hâte d'oublier!
Il fallait jeter à la mer ces années trompeuses,
pour ne plus retrouver, au quai, les heures creuses,
les navires cherchant leur chemin sous des étoiles connues,
et la soif de l'esprit comme une lame nue . . .

XI

I stopped in ports where hawkers
incited the spirit to a thirst for THINGS
their carpets' singing weave rewove
the taut African light.

That dry light floated like a canvas in the wind,
there was nothing human about it,
and yet I went ashore in a wide straw hat
to follow that inhuman song . . .

Strange, that song! Strange that thirst
I felt for the flesh of fruit that was anything but tender . . .

Uncertain afternoons!
I loved to lean across, like an angler,
your uncreated waters,
I was hoping for unknown fish, for light wonders,
for new balances
while the light turned circles around me
it climbed in my pockets, a happy lizard
so calm and so porous
was it searching for a lost secret of my substance?
We had the air of strangers who've danced at a ball
who lean an instant against each other
afraid to mix their sweat and their dreams,
while within them tremendous celebrations are taking place
wines without morning ring in their ears,
and a music rises like a hanging garden
—who in his learning wove the spider's web?
We were impatient to forget!
We had to throw those faithless years in the sea,
so at dockside we would not find, in our empty hours,
ships seeking their way beneath familiar stars,
and the spirit's thirst like an unsheathed blade . . .

La mort était somnolente, oublieuse,
oubliée nappe d'eau enfouie dans l'âme—
et SOUDAIN elle vint, elle coula en moi
comme le lait vivant dans le sein de la femme. ⁄

Death was somnolent, forgetful,
forgotten sheet of water deep in the soul—
and SUDDENLY it was there, it flowed in me
like living milk in a woman's breast.

XII

. . . dans la chair oubliée de l'homme, qui s'avance?
qui crie? qui sanglote?
Les routes sont tombées sur moi de tout leur long,
toutes les routes sont tombées . . .
Ortie du temps, où es-tu ma jolie?
Une envie est-ce peu,
une envie de crier, de pleurer,
de faire des trous dans l'eau fraîche,
au-dedans de moi une enfant sanglote sur mes genoux,
la route est longue et déchirée,
et je ne peux pas marcher et je ne peux pas chanter,
une chanson comme un soleil,
une chanson qui voudrait vivre,
une chanson qui ouvre l'œil
une chanson de cris et de balbutiements
—une chanson si bête, si bête . . .

Non, ce n'est pas cela,
c'est pas cela ni autre chose
c'est pas cela, bien sûr,
ni autre chose qui mûrit, qui ouvre en moi,
et qui est là et qui voudrait crier,
crier une parole longue,
un grand soleil de sable, un sanglot . . .

Cette nuit je suis seul avec ma lampe nue—
il n'y a pas de forêt à brûler,
rien à brûler, pas même un homme,
un homme, un homme et cependant . . .
Il y a de ces nuits que la tempête lave
un pas encore et l'eau jaillit sous tous les pas,
des nuits où quelque chose coule en moi,
monte jusqu'à ma gorge,
un fleuve monte

XII

. . . in man's forgotten flesh, who advances?
who cries out? who sobs?
The long roads fell on me with their whole length,
all the roads collapsed . . .
Nettle of time, where are you, pretty one?
Is a desire so small a thing,
a desire to shout, to cry,
to make holes in the cold water,
inside me a child is sobbing on my knees,
the road is long and torn up,
and I cannot walk and I cannot sing,
a song like a sun,
a song that yearns to live,
a song that opens the eye
a song of stammers and cries
—a song so dumb, so dumb . . .

No, that's not it
not that not something else
not that, of course,
nor something else that ripens, that opens in me
and that is there, and that yearns to shout,
to shout a long word,
great sun of sand, a sob . . .

Tonight I am alone with my bare lamp—
there is no forest to burn,
nothing to burn, not even a man,
a man, a man and yet . . .
There are such nights as these, washed by the storm
one step more and water streams from under every step,
nights when something flows inside me,
rises to my throat,
a river rises

une eau monte comme un couteau,
est-ce moi qui monte en moi-même
plus fort que moi, plus vaste,
moi-même comme une eau qui inonde une plaine,
moi-même sur le monde
et qui voudrais crier, qui voudrais sangloter
le monde . . .

Rien donc ne jaillira jusqu'au bord des paroles!
poissons dorés, poissons du cœur fêlé, paroles,
une chanson en moi, un sanglot,
un sanglot de plus dans le monde,
un sanglot qui noie le monde,
qui monte, qui monte et qui crie:
ASSEZ—ASSEZ et pas ASSEZ!
Pas assez de tout cela,
et cependant assez, assez, assez!
Pas assez de la mort,
et cependant assez de la vie!
Assez de tout, et pas assez de rien . . .

—Je vous donne ma mort, que vous en semble?
ma vie qu'en ferez-vous?
qu'est-ce ma vie?
une chanson un sanglot,
un sanglot tout petit dans les oreilles du monde,
un sanglot dans une forêt de sanglots . . .
Un sanglot—PAS ASSEZ!!!

Voici le monde—
si je pouvais le déchirer
si je pouvais me déchirer
moi-même sur le monde
debout et sanglotant
—sanglot le monde!
Si petit, si petit et si plein

water rises like a knife,
is it I who rise in myself
stronger than myself, vaster,
myself like water that inundates a plain,
myself over the world
who yearns to shout, who yearns to sob
the world . . .

So nothing will flood to the very edge of words!
fish of gold, fish of the broken heart, words,
a song within me, a sob,
just one more sob in the world,
a sob that drowns the world,
that rises, that rises and shouts:
ENOUGH—ENOUGH and not ENOUGH!
Not enough of all this,
and yet enough, enough, enough!
Not enough of death,
and yet enough of life!
Enough of everything, and not enough of nothing . . .

—I give you my death, what do you make of that?
what would you do with my life?
what is my life?
a song a sob
the smallest of sobs in the ears of the world
a sob in a forest of sobs . . .
A sob—NOT ENOUGH!!!

Here is the world—
if I could tear it apart
if I could tear myself apart
myself over the world
standing and sobbing
—the world a sob
So small, so small and so full

si plein, si plein et si petit,
si petit à pouvoir sangloter
si plein à pouvoir tout étreindre
un fleuve monte en moi, il monte,
je ne peux pas l'arrêter de mes mains
je ne peux pas l'empêcher de mon corps
—il passe à travers moi—il monte—

IL MONTE . . .

so full, so full and so small
so small that you could sob
so full that you would embrace it all
a river rises in me, it rises,
I can't stop it with my hands
I can't block it with my body
—it crosses me—rising—
RISING . . .

XIII

Un grain de terre m'eût suffi
qui m'a poussé dans les grand'villes?
Un grain de terre m'eût suffi—
qui m'a poussé dans les chaudières,
le corps dégingandé, les cuisses maigres,
le sang brûlé de fièvres,
lourd de mes testicules lourds?

Que ferais-je de ces bateaux,
de ces tempêtes, de ces eaux,
—du monde troué de hublots,
                    que ferais-je?

Une cale chargée de sacs de café, un wagon de troisième
plein de soldats puants et d'émigrants,
une vie sans escale,
une vie attachée à une roue et qui tourne,
avais-je assez marché et la guerre était devant,
assez marché, j'ai vu des régiments de sable,
marché—et on était ramassé par les routes
avec les chevaux fourbus et les camions défoncés,
loin du marché aux puces où mes aïeux sont morts
une prière sur les lèvres
à l'ombre d'une vieille bâtisse qui flanchait
—sous le poids de la vie—
barque de sauvetage qui avait trop servi.
Le soleil était là, c'était de la vieille ferraille,
enfant j'y ai joué—
pourquoi suis-je parti quand même,
qu'avais-je à espérer des routes,
c'est si calme une digue,
si reposant un seuil,
le jour y ouvre l'œil
sucré comme la figue,

XIII

A pinch of earth would have been enough
who thrust me into big cities?
A pinch of earth would have been enough—
who thrust me into the furnaces
my lanky body, my lean thighs
my blood burning with fever
heavy with my heavy testicles?

What could I possibly make of these boats,
these storms and these waters,
—what could I make of the world
                    full of portholes?

A ship's hold loaded with sacks of coffee, a third-class wagon
full of stinking soldiers and emigrants,
a life without going ashore,
a life tied to a turning wheel,
had I walked enough and war was still ahead,
walked enough, I saw regiments of sand,
walked—and we were gathered up by the roads
with broken horses and mangled trucks,
far from the flea market where my forebears died
a prayer on their lips
in the shade of an ancient farmhouse collapsed
—under the weight of life—
lifeboat used too many times.
The sun was there, it was a pile of scrap iron,
I played there as a child—
why did I leave,
what could I expect from the road,
a weir can be so calm,
a threshold so full of repose
day there opens its eye
sweet like a fig.

qu'avais-je encore à dire aux hommes,
ou qu'avais-je à attendre d'eux?
Parlons-nous donc la même langue—
brûlions-nous de la même soif?

. . . Ils poussaient la charrue dans la terre
ils avaient le regard de leurs bœufs: misérable et triste, rouge,
ils mettaient de côté le passé comme des philatélistes,
coude à coude, roseaux, ils empêchaient que l'étang ne bouge . . .

Que savaient-ils de la vie du toucheur dans les landes,
de la vie du manœuvre dans les marais salants,
de la vie du marin, tendue comme un arc que l'on bande,
de la vie du pêcheur de perles, aux poumons tendres,
—que savaient-ils de toi—de moi—perdus dans les sables mouvants? /

what did I have to say to men,
and what I was I expecting from them?
Do we really speak the same language—
did we burn with the same thirst?

. . . They guided the plow through the earth
they had the faces of their oxen: wretched, despondent, red,
they put aside the past like stamp collectors,
shoulder to shoulder, like reeds, they kept the pond in place . . .

What did they know of a herder's life on the moors,
of a laborer's life in the salt marshes,
of a sailor's life, bent like a bow being strung,
of the life of a pearl fisher with aching lungs,
—what did they know of you—of me—lost in quicksands?

XIV

—. . . Oui, j'ai aimé le monde:
—Combien de fois, soleil, te saluais-je
d'avoir hâlé ma transparence,
je m'étais couvert de ma voix,
je m'avançais dans le silence qui crissait,
j'aimais les forces, les écorces,
les bœufs qui touchent de leur front le vide,
les choses calmes, apaisantes, calmes,
les paysans la voix hâlée, la peau tannée,
la nappe tranquille du calme . . .
—le monde le voici
et me voici tout plein des morsures de l'air
le sang tourné, caillé,
dans ma chair une rixe invisible de coqs.
—Où aller?
J'ai appelé sur moi l'orage, le naufrage,
j'ai crié: nom de Dieu, j'ai frappé,
hagard, j'ai éventré le soleil,
j'étais ruisselant de sommeil,
par où commencer, où finir?
pourquoi ces questions se posent-elles?
que faudra-t-il haïr en fin de compte?
aimer était trop enfantin!
—Le monde est là, je m'y agrippe,
je m'accroche de mes deux mains,
je ne lâche pas cette proie,
je la marque de ma puissance,
je la couvre de mes empreintes!
J'étais en train de le modifier: je suis!
je n'avais pas perdu confiance,
la solitude n'était pas venue,
le dégoût ni l'ennui n'étaient là . . .

XIV

. . . Yes, I loved the world:
—How often did I hail you, sun,
for having tanned my transparency,
I covered myself with my voice,
I walked through the screeching silence
I loved forces and the bark of trees,
oxen that touch their foreheads to the void,
calm things, soothing, calm,
peasants with suntanned voices, leathery skin,
the tranquil sheet of calm . . .
—here is the world
and here I am, bitten by the air
my blood gone sour, curdled,
an invisible cockfight in my flesh.
—Where can I go?
I called the storm, the shipwreck, down on myself,
I shouted: by God, I struck out,
haggard, I gutted the sun,
I was dripping with sleep,
where to start, where to end?
why do these questions arise?
what in the end must we hate?
love was for children!
—The world is there, I catch hold,
I grip it with both my hands,
I won't let this prey escape,
I mark it with my force,
I cover it with my prints!
I was altering it: I exist!
I had not lost confidence,
solitude hadn't arrived,
neither disgust nor boredom was there . . .

—Ne rien pouvoir tenir en mains voilà la fin . . .
. . . Sous les paupières closes y avait-il des yeux?
Mes mains s'étaient fermées sur leur propre creux.
Mes mains étaient vides bien sûr,
j'avais aimé, j'avais haï le vide
inutile de sangloter,
au bout de moi-même MOI-MÊME,
toujours moi-même, plein de bave, plein de lave
moi-même dans le Temps
plein de besoins plein d'appétits
plus grande ma soif que le monde
plus grande ma faim que le monde,
pas de chanson, pas d'échanson,
personne de qui espérer du secours,
nul Dieu sanglotant ou féroce,
qui prier, qui frapper au visage,
nulle voix apaisante, désaltérante,
nul visage . . .

—Unable to keep my hands on something, this is the end . . .
. . . Under the closed eyelids, were there eyes?
My hands were cupped around their own hollowness.
My hands of course were empty,
I had loved, I had hated the void
useless to sob
at the end of myself MYSELF,
always myself, slavering, seething
myself in Time,
full of needs full of desires
my thirst greater than the world
my hunger greater than the world,
no song, no cup bearer,
I could not hope for help,
no God, sobbing or fierce,
that I might pray to, that I might strike his face
no soothing, nourishing voice,
no face . . .

XV

Tu avais une déesse à tes côtés, Ulysse!
—À quoi sert-il de voyager?
Une jarre de lait calme, les cuisses de l'épouse,
les jours comme des pommes tombées dans le verger,
une belle lumière lisse,
la paix de l'œuvre faite et la nuit à l'auberge,
vieillir tout doucement près d'un pichet de vin
quand la lune blanchit le large,
tout en trinquant avec des marins revenus
infirmes, d'on ne sait quelles batailles louches
qu'on a du mal à épeler . . .
—À quoi sert-il de s'en aller
déjà vaincu, avant d'avoir ouvert la bouche,
dans des pays d'où l'on ne reviendra que vieux
plein de sirènes que l'on n'a pas écoutées
de victoires manquées
et le cœur lourd d'avoir résisté à sa soif?

XV

Ulysses, you had a goddess at your side!
—What good is the voyage?
A pitcher of still milk, the spouse's thighs,
days like apples fallen in the orchard,
a fine mellowed light,
the peace of a job well done and nights at the tavern,
aging slowly beside a jug of wine
as the moon whitens the open sea,
and toasting with sailors who have returned
crippled, from who knows what fishy battles
with names that are hard to spell . . .
—What good is going off
already beaten before you have opened your mouth
to countries you will return from only old
carrying sirens that went unheeded
victories that slipped away
a heavy heart from having resisted your thirst?

XVI

Le monde est fini, le voyage
commence.
Y a-t-il encore un soleil
quelque part?

Nous avons peur de la vie,
nous avons peur de la mort,
de toutes ces vieilles chansons
de nourrice.

Nous portons avec nous
le poids d'une race d'ancêtres
qui ont trop aimé cette terre
pour ne pas la haïr.

Nous sommes issus de la pierre
lourde et sauvage,
nous fûmes des rocs, des racines,
jamais oiseaux, jamais nuages—
feuilles des cimes—

Les dieux ah! sont morts.
Nous cherchons
des hommes. Des hommes
qui n'aient pas peur d'achever
ce qui reste des dieux.

XVI

The world ends, the voyage
is only beginning.
Somewhere out there
is there still a sun?

We are afraid of life,
we are afraid of death
and all the old
nursery rhymes.

We carry with us
the weight of a race of ancestors
who loved this earth too much
not to hate it.

We are descended from heavy
and rugged stone,
we were always rocks, and roots,
never birds, never clouds—
topmost leaves—

The gods, ah! are dead.
We are seeking
men. Men who are not
afraid to finish off
what's left of the gods.

XVII

Je largue les amarres qui me tiennent lié à la terre,
l'arc-en-ciel qui m'attache à tous les autres hommes,
les bandages qui cousent ma plaie aux autres plaies,
je quitte le lit des vivants,
les grandes voix des morts aux racines terribles
les photos de famille sur le métal des foires
et le ventre où m'attend le nouveau-né du cœur.
Voici la vérité, je suis seul,
seul dans ma propre nuit où mon ombre se couche
dans la chose qui fuit je me touche et me perds
égoutier du grand songe,
ma main me pousse pleine de lignes, de racines,
—ai-je vraiment manqué de foi?
Je grimpe les Alpes de force et je n'ai pas de guide
je ne suis pas alpiniste,
je n'ai pas demandé le danger, il est là,
je n'aime pas marcher, qui est-ce qui marche en moi?
—S'était-on trompé de personne?
Je hais le vide et voilà qu'il sonne en mon poème.
Je cogne un front têtu contre les cimes d'air
je ne suis pas un héros—
les applaudissements me gênent, qu'en ferais-je?
les hyènes me suivent de leur regard en brosse:
qui leur a dit que je serai cadavre un jour?
. . . Tout seul je suis la route humaine; à qui la route?
à qui les mots déjà inventés avant moi?
Dans la bouche des femmes d'anciens baisers rassis
dorment sur les gencives,
tout seul j'arrache le secret, bribe par bribe,
tout seul je sème et je moissonne l'homme,
j'avance dans les villes absurdes où tout m'étonne,
dans les boulangeries le pain ouvrait les yeux,
le cri du pauvre monte à la gorge de Dieu,

XVII

I cast off the ropes that hold me fast to the earth,
the rainbow that joins me to other men,
the bandage that stitches my wound to other wounds,
I leave the bed of the living,
the great voices of the grim-rooted dead
the family photos against the metal of fairs
the womb where the newborn of the heart awaits me.
This is the truth, I am alone,
alone in my private night where my shadow goes to bed
I touch and I lose myself in the thing that flees
sewage worker of the great dream,
my hand urges me, full of lines, of roots,
—have I really lacked faith?
I scale the Alps by force without a guide
I am no mountaineer,
I did not ask for danger, but there it is,
I don't like walking, who is walking in me?
—Maybe there was a mistake?
I hate the void and yet it rings in my poem.
I knock my stubborn forehead against the heights of air
I am no hero—
applause embarrasses me, what would I do with it?
the hyenas track me with their crew-cut gaze:
who told them I'll be a corpse one day?
. . . Alone, I am the human road; whose road?
whose are the words invented before me?
Stale kisses sleep on the gums
in women's mouths,
alone I drag out the secret, piece by piece,
alone I sow and harvest man,
I walk through absurd cities where everything is a surprise,
the bread in bakeries opened my eyes
. the cry of the poor rises in the throat of God,

à l'hôpital au moins les murs seront très blancs,
la lumière sera assise à table, vieille,
dans ma voix les lavandières auront des jambes d'eau
    si nous entrions danser
    dans la pharmacie ouverte,
    si nous nous laissions flotter
    sur la crème de l'étang,
le temps sera enfin troué par les orties,
soleil voudras-tu être aussi de la partie,
    soleil méchant qui chauffe
    l'or et la pourriture
    le vide qui sanglote
    dans les paroles mûres.

    Il n'y a pas de vide,
    pourquoi me tourmenter?
Je vous donne mes mains, je vous donne mon ombre—
il n'y a pas de vide et je suis seul au monde.

at the hospital at least the walls will be so white,
the light will sit down to eat, grown old,
in my voice the legs of the washerwomen will be of water
    suppose we went to dance
    in the open pharmacy,
    suppose we let ourselves float
    on the cream of the pond,
nettles at last would make holes in time,
sun do you also want to join the game,
    malicious sun that heats
    gold and rot alike
    the void sobbing
    in ripened words.

    There is no such things as the void,
    so why do I torment myself?
I give you my hands, I give you my shadow—
There is no such thing as the void, and I am alone in the world.

XVIII

Les paroles devraient se presser dans ma bouche
comme naguère . . . Quand? Je me souviens à peine . . .
Mais qu'importe les quais où l'on charge
le môle où l'on s'embarque
avec les dames blanches qui hantent les châteaux
des Sénégalais au nez plat
de grosses filles pour le commerce
une petite institutrice de Bretagne
fermée dans sa coquille—
et quelques disques dont on mâchera la rengaine
sous les paupières du tropique . . .
Ce soir, la mer s'embête et boude . . .
Quelle fêlure veut-elle donc oublier,
gonflée de ta laitance amère, solitude?
—Qui donc l'empêche de crier
échevelée, exsangue,
de percer les bateaux d'émigrants et d'y passer la langue,
de tremper le mouchoir des voiliers dans l'onde,
de lécher l'agonie salée des mariniers,
de cracher au visage insolent du monde
—Qui donc l'empêche de prier,
de mendier un peu de soleil pour beurrer sa peau,
de baiser les noyés sur la bouche,
de lessiver tendrement le sommeil des poissons?
—Qui donc l'empêche de parier,
de jeter le clinquant de sa vie éternelle
sur le tapis vert des dieux—
trouer l'opacité des dieux,
et demander aux grandes ténèbres qui l'attirent:
—qui donc m'empêche de mourir?

XVIII

Words should rush in my mouth
as once they did . . . When? I can hardly remember . . .
But never mind the docks where they are loading
the jetty where they are boarding
with the white ladies who haunt old castles
flat-nosed Senegalese
stout girls for commerce
a little Breton teacher
closed in her shell—
and a few records whose played-out tunes we'll chew on
under the eyelids of tropical zones . . .
This evening the sea is sullen and bored . . .
What flaw is it striving to forget,
swollen, solitude, with your bitter roe?
—Who keeps it from crying out
disheveled, drained of blood
from piercing the boats of emigrants and slipping its tongue in,
from wetting with swell the handkerchiefs of sailboats,
from licking the salty agony of sailors,
from spitting in the insolent face of the world
—Who keeps it from praying,
from begging a little sun to grease its skin,
from kissing the drowned on the lips,
from gently laundering the sleep of fish?
—Who keeps it from gambling,
from flinging the sparkle of its eternal life
on the gaming table of the gods—
from making holes in the opacity of the gods
and asking the great shadows that beckon:
—so who keeps me from dying?

XIX

Les paysages vus dans les caisses des mers
l'aube sale des ports aux soleils futurs
je m'avance à travers la ville libre,
inconnu, inconnu, où irai-je, où vas-tu
parmi les détritus d'oranges, de fatigues,
j'arrive et te voilà, tu es vieille Amérique,
je te trouve saleté
visage familier de la boîte aux ordures,
naissance de la race ouvrière au matin
le pain n'est plus déjà qu'une lueur de pain
la faim est là qui triche . . .
mais les affiches parlent de fêtes crapuleuses,
affiche de meetings, de grèves, de saisies,
de bals à l'Opéra, de films en Malaisie,
de songes et d'émeutes
—suis-je vraiment celui qu'on attend pour la fête,
dois-je montrer mes reins,
dois-je crier à tue-tête
quels sont les fruits nouveaux dont vous avez besoin
quel est le paradis qu'il vous plairait de perdre
je ne sais pas la langue que vous parlez qu'y puis-je?
je ne suis pas chiromancien,
mes mots, mes maux sont ceux de tout le monde,
je n'ai rien inventé de nouveau, d'ancien,
la terre si petite, le voyage si long,
plus grande notre soif que celle de Colomb!
J'avais assez de suivre l'Europe aux fesses creuses,
n'avez-vous pas d'autres résines, d'autres crises,
la même chose et cependant
un verre de gros rouge sur les comptoirs de l'aube,
un peu de bon tabac
pour rouler une sèche?
Vos rues m'ont attrapé comme lassos, où vais-je,

XIX

Landscapes glimpsed in the packing crates of the seas,
the sullied dawns of ports by the light of suns to come
I walk through the free city,
unknown, unknown, where will I go, where are you going
amid the orange rinds, the exhaustion,
I arrive and there you are, you are old, America,
I find you filth
familiar face from the trash bin,
birth of the working class at morning
already bread is less than the glimmer of bread
cheating hunger is there . . .
but the posters speak of low-life carnivals,
posters for meetings, for strikes, for confiscations,
for Opera balls, for films set in Malaysia
for dreams and riots
—am I really the one they're waiting for to begin the party?
must I bare the small of my back,
must I shout at the top of my voice
what are the novel fruits you need
what is the paradise that you would like to lose
I do not speak your language, what can I do?
I am no palm reader,
my words, my ills, are the same as any man's,
I've invented nothing new, or old,
the world is so small, the voyage so long,
our thirst greater than Columbus's!
I had followed long enough the sunken ass of Europe,
do you have no other resins, no other crises,
the same thing and yet
a glass of rough red wine on the counters of dawn,
a bit of good tobacco
to roll a smoke?
Your streets ensnared me like a lasso, where am I going,

où sont vos mains d'amis, pourquoi ces flèches,
personne n'est venu vers moi, le regard bleu.

Les murs sont pleins d'ennui, le linge tendu sèche
—que faites-vous de votre soleil?
Laissez-moi m'en couper un morceau saignant!
Terres silencieuses, peaux-rouges océanes,
que le maïs est triste au plat de vos savanes,
quelles amours cherché-je dans vos quartiers infâmes
de quelle odeur humaine ai-je espéré le sel?
J'ai beau mêler mon cœur au vôtre, je suis seul,
avais-je quelque chose à vous dire?
J'ai un si grand besoin de rire, de pleurer,
qui veut donner la joie à un marchand d'épaves,
quelle femme qui me suivrait à l'hôtel
pour dix minutes de caresses sourdes?
J'ai tant de vie en moi qui voudrait sourdre,
tant de moulins à vent qui voudraient moudre
—j'espérais un pays de choses minérales,
dois-je porter mon nom comme une enseigne usée
de vieille auberge médusée?
—Aidez-moi donc à m'oublier!
Plus tard je vous paierai en charmes, en sanglots,
je suis venu vers vous, l'écorce tendre
aidez-moi donc à la durcir!
aidez-moi, aidez-moi à devenir un autre.

where is your friendly hand, why these arrows,
no one came to me with blue in his eyes.

The walls are full of weariness, the laundry stretched dry
—what do you do with your sun?
Let me cut myself a dripping-red piece!
Silent lands, red-skinned women of the coasts,
the corn on your flat savannas is so dreary,
what loves was I seeking in your quarters of vice
hoping to find the salt of what human smell?
For all I mingle my heart with yours, I am alone,
did I have something to tell you?
I feel such need to laugh, to cry,
and who has pleasure to give to a dealer of shipwrecks,
what woman who would follow me to the hotel
for ten minutes of muffled caress?
I have so much life in me that yearns to surge
so many windmills yearning to grind
—I had hoped for a land of mineral things,
must I wear my name like the worn-off sign
of an ancient dumbstruck tavern?
—So help me forget myself!
I will pay you back later, in charms, in sobs,
I approached you with tender bark
so help me harden!
help me, help me become another.

XX

La terre a trop de bœufs ce matin sur ses épaules
elle se déchausse pour courir, crache ses eaux minérales,
elle aime labourer les trains et les mécaniciens,
elle aime broyer la mélancolie des déraillements anciens,
tout ce qui fut vitesse, cœur, cri, marche et bielle—
enfoui à présent sous la fiente du sang et du temps.

XX

The land this morning has shouldered too many oxen
it kicks off its shoes to run, spits mineral waters,
it likes to plow under mechanics and trains, it likes
to crush the melancholy of old derailments,
all that was speed, heart, cry and connecting rod—
all buried now under droppings of blood and time.

XXI

J'avançais dans la foule, nul ne savait mon nom,
—l'eussent-ils su, quelle importance?
Moi-même le savais-je? Et je tournais en rond,
saoulé par les lumières noires,
comme si cette foule était le vent du large,
comme si quelque chose pouvait venir de là,
houleuse, indifférente,
comme si les têtards qui grouillaient dans la vase
de ce port inhumain
étaient des hommes et non des rescapés craintifs
de vieux naufrages innommables,
des déchets d'une fête ancienne, oubliée,
des paquets d'appétits, de pus, de solitude,
de choses grelottantes, ah!

On s'était rencontré quelque part, c'était sûr,
dans quelque queue humaine à l'aube, il bruinait
—pour un pain, ou pour un visa, c'était long,
c'était long la guerre, la paix,
longue et sordide l'aube,
et cette découverte du rien, si lente, oh!
et ce malaise au cœur plus lourd qu'une grossesse
l'humiliation d'être rien,
des émigrants sans passeport,
de nul peuple, d'aucun pays,
chacun parlant une autre langue,
la langue de sa petite vie obscure,
la langue d'un désir de pain, de destruction,
de tendresse, de miel, de songe, de puissance,
d'un toit avec une fraîcheur dans le lit . . .
Et j'étais parmi eux parlant ma propre langue
que je ne comprenais plus, ah!
Et j'avançais craignant qu'on m'oubliât et je criais
de peur, de faim, d'angoisse:

92 ⮜ BENJAMIN FONDANE

XXI

I walked through the crowd, and no one knew my name
—yet had they known, what difference would that have made?
Did I know myself? I turned in circles,
drunk on the black lights,
as if that crowd was wind from the open sea,
as if something could reach us from there,
whipped up, indifferent,
as if the swarms of tadpoles in the muck of that
inhuman port
were men, and not those scared survivors
of old, unnameable shipwrecks,
that trash from a party over and forgotten,
bundles of puss, and appetite, and solitude,
of shivering things, ah!

We had met before, somewhere, that much is sure,
waiting in line at dawn, in a fine rain
—for bread, for a visa, it was long,
the war was long, and peace,
dawn long and sordid
and that discovery of nothing was so slow, oh!
that pain in the chest heavier than pregnancy
the indignity of being nothing at all,
emigrants without passports,
a people or a country,
each speaking a different tongue,
the language of his own small bounded life
the language of desire for bread, for destruction
for tenderness, honey, dream, for force,
a roof above and a freshness in bed . . .
And I was with them speaking my own language
which I no longer understood, ah!
And I stepped forward, afraid I had been forgotten, and I cried out
from fear, from hunger, from dread:

«Moi aussi . . . moi aussi, je suis un dieu. Pitié!»
—Cela faisait un bruit de crécelle éraillée,
un aigre filet de musique,
une plainte cassée qui traversait l'histoire,
qui roulait, qui roulait, roulait hors de l'histoire
. . . Hors de l'histoire . . . oui . . . !

"And I . . . I too am a god. Have pity!"
—Which made the noise of a scratchy rattle,
a shrill and tinny music
a broken plaint that crossed history,
that rolled, that rolled, rolled beyond history,
. . . Beyond history . . . yes . . . !

XXII

Aucune importance, bien sûr,
que je fusse dans la rue, dans un ventre,
ou dans l'œil mort de cette chambre,
seul dans l'aquarium du monde,
attendant quelque chose que je savais déjà
impossible, impossible,
et pourtant souhaité au-delà du possible,
un visage, une main,
une sonnette prise soudain de tremblement,
un bruit de pas, de voix montant dans le silence
comme la crue houleuse d'une rivière en mars
—terrible, violente!
— . . . Mais est-ce donc si important,
cela fera-t-il une date,
un digne événement de l'Histoire moderne,
si quelqu'un se trompait d'escalier, de porte,
et apportait, ne fût-ce que pour un rien de temps,
une poignée d'odeur humaine
à ce gardien de phare quasi fou de terreur?

XXII

Of course it is of no importance
whether I was in the street, or in a womb,
or in the dead eye of this room,
alone in the aquarium of the world,
waiting for something I knew already
to be impossible, impossible and yet
hoped for beyond all possibility,
a face, a hand,
a doorbell suddenly seized by trembling,
the sound of steps, voices rising in the silence
like the furious rise of a river in March
—violent, terrible!
— . . . But then is it so important,
would it make a date,
an event worthy of Modern History,
if someone mistook the stairwell, the door,
and brought, even for just a moment,
a handful of human smell
to this lighthouse keeper nearly mad from fear?

XXIII
Amérique, Amérique . . .

à Victoria Ocampo

Amérique, Amérique, merveille noire et rouge,
que de fois j'ai rêvé de tes chevaux sauvages
que de fois l'œil plus clair d'être ouvert en dedans
tes fleuves m'ont porté, humide, dans tes flancs,
ô vierge, encore nue depuis ta découverte!
—Puissé-je être celui qui causera ta perte!
Puisses-tu arrêter de ne pas finir!
Que n'y a-t-il encore un monde à découvrir
maille après maille!

Amérique du Sud ouverte en éventail
dans la paume fermée de la Terre de Feu
(il suffit d'un regard amoureux sur la mappe)
j'aime tes plaines pacifiques
tes nappes inhumaines
tes grands ports où l'on dort le regard sous l'eau
tes Indiens anachroniques
ramant sans bruit le long de tes méditations
tes plantations où l'homme s'enfonce jusqu'au cou
tes émeutes soudaines
tes matinées paresseuses et ta lumière trouble
tes nuages énormes et tes ombú géants
ta pampa infinie,
tes longs serpents mûris par leur venin de mort . . .
—Dans tes ports j'ai flâné longtemps, le rêve au ventre . . .
Marchand, marchand qui n'avait rien à vendre
je trafiquais la destruction,
je te voyais de loin le visage tranquille,
tes jeunes seins de vieille fille,
Amérique du Sud entourée de mers
continent sans mémoire

XXIII
America, America . . .

for Victoria Ocampo

America, America, black and red wonder,
how often did I dream of your wild horses
how often, the eye more lucid from within,
did your rivers bear me sweating down your side?
O virgin, naked ever since you were found!
—May I be the one who dishonors you!
May you stop stretching on without end!
That there were not another world to discover
woven mile by mile!

South America opening like a fan
in the closed palm of Tierra del Fuego
(one loving look at the map is enough)
I love your pacific plains
your inhuman sheets
your great ports where men sleep with their gaze underwater
your anachronistic Indians
silently rowing the length of your meditations
your plantations where man is buried up to the neck
your sudden riots
your lazy mornings and your murky light
your enormous clouds, your giant ombú
your endless Pampas,
your serpents ripened on their deadly venom . . .
—I wandered long in your ports, a dream in my gut . . .
Merchant, merchant with nothing to sell
I trafficked in destruction,
I saw you from afar, your face at ease,
your young breasts of an old maid,
South America surrounded by seas
continent without memory

ouvrage improvisé par des soldats cruels
l'œil fier sur un cheval de pierre dans tes villes—

j'ai baisé ton ennui aux cils de tes bordels,
j'ai partagé vos lourdes tristesses, sang-mêlé,
et ce mal du pays des gens qui n'en ont plus.
J'ai foulé tes pavés, j'ai rêvé dans tes rues,
tes hommes longuement m'émeuvent . . .
Que ne puis-je rester un instant sur tes rives,
enfoncer mes racines dans une terre neuve,
naviguer tout au long des côtes du connu,
me lier d'amitié avec ta terre épaisse,
couvert de tes moutons qui ont la laine lasse.
—Amérique, ta terre est vaste!
Aie pitié de ces pauvres et sales émigrants
qui se déplacent, lents, avec leurs dieux anciens!
Je suis un étranger, je le sais.
Je n'ai pas de patrie collée à mes souliers,
plus rien qui me retienne à quelque quai du vide . . .
Puisses-tu me mener en laisse par la main!
puisses-tu apaiser mon pauvre cœur d'Asie!
N'es-tu pas une terre absurde, une oasis,
un pays de chevaux libres de toute bride?

. . . oubli de tout, de rien . . . Nuages d'Amérique!

hack job improvised by savage soldiers
with proud expressions on stone horses in your cities—

I kissed your weariness on your brothels' lashes,
I shared the heavy sadness of your mixed blood,
and the homesickness of those without a home.
I trod your paving stones, I dreamed in your streets,
your men move me a long time . . .
Why can't I stay a moment on your shores,
sink my roots in a new land,
sail up and down the coasts of the known,
strike up friendship with your thick land,
blanketed with your sheep, with their tired wool?
—America, your land is wide!
Pity these emigrants who arrive
dirty and tired with their ancient gods.
I am a stranger here, I know.
I have no homeland stuck to my shoes,
nothing that holds me back on some dock of the void . . .
May you lead me by the hand, on a leash!
May you soothe my poor heart of Asia!
Are you not an oasis, an absurd land,
a country of horses free from every rein?

. . . forgetting all, or nothing . . . Clouds of America!

XXIV

. . . et l'Argentine. La pampa était à gauche,
cela faisait de la poussière sur les hommes.
Chaque jour je prenais une rue inconnue
avec l'espoir d'y arriver
seul le désert avait de quoi calmer ma soif
j'avais besoin d'un monde sans horizon ni fin
d'un monde plat, de sables,
j'avais un grand besoin d'étouffer
de changer de température,
donnez-moi un pays qui soit à ma mesure
pareil au vieux chaos
avec de l'herbe amère et des soleils sauvages
des hommes lents et dangereux
des taureaux immobiles
s'acharnant de leur front contre le calme plat
—pampa, pampa, où mon désir rampa,
je rêvais d'avancer dans ton regard immense,
toucher l'infini de mes coudes
pourquoi tant de terre suivie de terres et de terres
sans vagues ni écume
que te voulais-je, solitude,
puisses-tu ne pas arrêter de couler,
source ardente!
Mon cœur était plus vide que toi et plus brûlant,
des chardons y poussaient, fruits de la sécheresse
les oiseaux étaient pleins de sommeil
quel ennui portaient-ils sous leurs ailes lasses
un nuage touchait ma tête—
l'amour, l'amour était aussi vaste, aussi bête,
il fallait s'y livrer à plein corps,
il fallait s'y livrer jusqu'à en perdre haleine . . .

XXIV

. . . and Argentina. The Pampas was on the left,
stirring up dust on the men.
Each day I tried an unfamiliar street
hoping to find it
only the desert had what it took to calm my thirst
I needed a world without horizon or end
a flat world of sands,
I desperately needed a stifling heat
a change in temperature,
give me a country that's fit for me
resembling the old chaos
with bitter grass and untamed suns
slow and dangerous men
motionless bulls
butting their foreheads against the flat calm
—Pampas, Pampas, where my desire crawled forward
I dreamed of walking through your vast gaze,
of touching the infinite with my elbows
why so much land followed by lands and lands
with neither wave nor foam
what did I want from you, solitude,
may you never stop flowing,
fervent spring!
My heart burned hotter and was emptier than you,
thistles grew there, fruit of the dryness
the birds were filled with sleep
what boredom did they carry on their tired wings
a cloud brushed my head—
and love, and love was just as wide and just as dumb,
we had to throw our whole bodies into it,
we had to give ourselves up, till we were breathless . . .

XXV

. . . mais il y a longtemps que ça se passe ainsi.
La caissière sourit au fond de la boucherie
comme le noyau roux dans l'amande
—est-elle petite, est-elle grande?
Les hommes pondent dans la viande fraîche,
ils pullulent sur les viandes, sur les graisses,
ils travaillent dans les égouts, dans la vidange;
d'aucuns gagnent leur pain dans ces métiers étranges:
sinistres, grêles, catastrophes, bris de glaces,
pompes funèbres.

Depuis longtemps la mort avance dans vos mains,
elle est cachée par le journal qu'un monsieur lit dans le train,
c'est le voisin de pissotière, dont on ne voit que les jambes,
au cinéma elle est sur l'écran, c'est une «vamp»,
tu cherches ses genoux, vos visages se touchent,
et le sanglot soudain mûrit entre vos bouches.

Dans le sommeil, on ne sait où,
le soleil tourne dans un trou.
Soleil cuis-moi, mûris ma chair comme un concombre,
j'ai renoncé tu sais, j'ai accroché mon ombre,
la mer peut désormais s'en aller
toute seule.

Je te hais, te caresse et te vomis angoisse,
la terre reste mais l'eau passe, valse,
porté au plus haut de la houle
je crie: quelle vague me roule?
Je ne sais pas la route, il n'y a pas de route
—pourquoi me suis-je donc confié à la mer?

XXV

. . . but this way of things is nothing new.
The cashier smiles from the back of the butcher's shop
like the almond's russet stone—
is she short, is she tall?
Men lay their eggs on fresh meat,
they swarm on the meats and fats,
they work in sewers and drains;
some earn their bread in these strange professions:
disasters, hail, catastrophes, broken glass,
funerals.

Death has long been advancing in your hands,
hid by the paper a man is reading on the train,
it's the next fellow at the urinal, whose legs alone can be seen,
at movies it's on the screen, it's a "vamp,"
you seek its knees, your faces touch,
and the sudden sob ripens between your mouths.

In sleep, who knows where,
the sun goes down a lair.
Roast me, sun, ripen my flesh like a cucumber,
I have renounced, you know, I've hung up my shadow,
henceforth the sea can go on
alone.

I hate and caress and vomit you, dread,
the land remains but water passes, waltzes,
carried to the highest point of the swell, I shout:
what wave is taking me for a ride?
I do not know the road, there is no road—
so why did I trust myself to the sea?

XXVI

Fleur de neige
fleur de bruit
fleur de braise
fleur de truite,
où sommes-nous depuis que la clarté tomba
(avec, dans notre sang, la fatigue des loups)
—à la recherche de quels commerces?
—aux racines de quelles sources?
le désir allumé au phosphore des nerfs . . .

L'aube n'est pas encore, il s'en faut
—La lampe brûle,
à quoi bon s'appuyer aux choses qui s'écroulent,
il est beaucoup de vies qui ont brûlé pour rien,
beaucoup de vies qui ont honte.
—Dormirais-je, dormirez-vous?
. . . étoiles de la fin du monde!
. . . Que ne puis-je me mettre au chaud sous mon sommeil,
que ne peut-on ôter son visage de jour
—et dormir sans figure!

XXVI

Flower of snow
flower of noise
flower of embers
flower of trout,
since twilight fell, where are we?
(feeling in our blood the fatigue of wolves)
—in search of what exchange?
—at the roots of what springs?
desire illuminated by our phosphorescent nerves . . .

Dawn has not come yet, it is still far
—The lamp burns,
what good is leaning on things that crumble,
there are so many lives that burned for naught,
so many lives ashamed.
—Will I be able to sleep, will you?
. . . stars of the end of the earth!
. . . Why can I not take shelter in the warmth of sleep,
why can't we remove our masks of day
—and sleep without a face?

XXVII

aux confins de la vie et la mort nous avons vu
la camomille tendre des lampes des bordels

. . . te souviens-tu de la petite
peau-rouge qu'on avait lancée
comme une truite dans un bouge
seize ans, mais si bien balancée
que l'eau nous venait à la bouche?

Dieu! quel regard de fond des bois
dans cette fillette aux abois!

Elle débutait ce soir-là
mais s'est donnée sans une plainte.
Comme le temps passe et s'en va
que reste-t-il de cette étreinte?
. . . sa bouche était à peine peinte
Que de mers, que de sel et que de solitudes
que de regards qui traînent dans l'œil comme un nuage
avions-nous parcourus, compagnons! Et soudain
au fond de la lumière des villes, sanglotants,
pareils au liseron qui cherche des tuteurs
pour s'agripper et n'accroche que des tuteurs fantômes:
ces pays, ces oasis pour les fièvres du sang
et pour les violences sans bride!
Nulle part, plus que là, l'angoisse d'être seuls
ne nous poignait autant, la prière sans dieu,
et la tendresse non partagée et la soif
restée entière. Longue et si atroce soif
d'humain, inapaisée, inapaisante, unique.

. . . te souviens-tu, Ungaretti,
de notre nuit sur le tropique
à Bahia-de-tous-les-saints?
Au carrefour des trois églises

XXVII

at the ends of life and death we saw
the gentle chamomile of brothel lamps

. . . do you remember the
little redskin tossed
like a trout in a dive
only sixteen, but so well built
she made our mouths water?

God, what look of the deep forest
in the eyes of that girl at bay!

That evening was her first
but she gave herself without complaint.
As time passes and flees
what's left of that embrace?
 . . . her lips were barely painted
What seas, what salt and what solitudes
what gazes floating in the eye like a cloud
have we crossed, companions! And suddenly
in the depths of city lights, sobbing,
like a morning-glory vine that searches the air for a stake
to grow on and grasps at only the ghosts of stakes:
these lands, these oases for fevered blood
and unbridled violence!
Nowhere else did we feel the stab
of loneliness so deeply, the godless prayer,
tenderness unshared and thirst
that stayed intact. Long and atrocious thirst
for something human, unquenched, unquenching, unique.

. . . Ungaretti, do you remember
our night in the tropics
at All-Saints' Bay?
At the crossroads of three churches

une jeune négresse marchait dans nos regards
on ne voyait que le tremblement de ses fesses
qu'on eût pu prendre dans la main,
elle jouait des hanches c'était une putain,
elle était tiède et trouble en dedans comme le lait dans une noix de coco
que n'étions-nous des matelots,
nous l'aurions ouverte au couteau comme une huître
nous nous serions saoulés pour l'oublier ensuite.

Fausses beautés qui tant troublèrent notre chair
fausses beautés qui tant, un jour, nous furent chères
pénélopes usées, juliettes avachies
—aviez-vous eu pitié du voyageur? A-t-il
eu pitié de vos chairs molles et misérables
ô mal-aimées? flottant sur l'eau comme des algues
sœurs des brouillards verdâtres et des fanaux douteux
—vies sans importance!
—parapluies oubliés!
est-il jamais venu quelqu'un vous réclamer
au bureau des vies perdues?

Chairs sans désirs créées pour le sang chaud, les fièvres basses
chairs vénérables entre toutes les chairs,
—nuques sans rêve!
Nous avons vu les sales grabats des quartiers bas,
le sommeil des poitrines pesantes sur les tables,
les bouches roses et pâteuses,
le cauchemar gonflait, ballon d'enfant, gonflait,
que notre vie, que la musique, étaient creuses,
ô puisses-tu ne pas t'y trouver, Nausicaà!

. . . Louches maisons marines!
On y poussait d'abord son ombre et l'on entrait
ça sentait le moisi et le crime

—TERRE PROMISE

a black girl was walking in our gaze
we saw nothing but her shaking haunches
we could have taken it in our hands,
she played her hips, she was a whore,
she was warm and turbid inside like the milk in a coconut
why were we not sailors
we would have opened her up with a knife like an oyster
we would have drunk our fill then forgotten her.

False beauties who so inflamed our flesh
false beauties who once were so dear
worn Penelopes, sagging Juliets
—did you take pity on the traveler? Did he
pity your soft and sorry flesh,
O lovelorn ones? floating like seaweed on the swell
sisters of greenish fog and faithless lanterns
—lives without importance!
—umbrellas left behind!
has anyone ever come to claim you
at the office of lost lives?

Impassive flesh created for hot blood and low fevers
flesh revered of all flesh,
—napes without dreams!
We saw the dirty cots of those seedy districts,
the sleep of heavy chests leaning on tables,
the pink and pasty mouths,
the nightmare swelled, as a child's ball, swelled,
our lives, the music, were so hollow,
O may you never end up there, Nausicaa!

. . . Sleazy sailors' houses!
First we pushed our shadows in, then went in ourselves
it smelled of mildew and crime

—PROMISED LAND

Je t'ai connue avant l'amour, après l'amour
j'avais mal aux entrailles quand je montais tes marches
l'aube saignait déjà aux gencives des jours,
un disque las jouait une romance vache

—amère parodie du paradis perdu
ta lumière était malsaine!
Fins de semaine, longues telle une robe à traîne,
le phare nous lavait, barques abandonnées,
des femmes étaient là, de toutes les contrées,
masses de viande avec une rose aux cheveux
l'amour était selon la race,
des matelots avaient passé par-là, des débardeurs,
la violence avait passé par-là, la poisse,
dans ces peaux les cheminées avaient jeté leur cri
les cordages s'étaient mêlés aux chevelures
quels voyages! avec l'orage et le roulis,
sur ces seins on sentait, lourd et gras,
le pis rose des vaches et des mères lointaines
ça fleurait la peau douce de la petite sœur,
chairs délicates, chairs de la sœur, de la mère
chairs vénérables entre toutes les chairs
terres promises!

aux confins de la vie de la mort—*promises.*

I knew you before love, and after love
my stomach turned as I went up the steps
dawn bled already on the gums of days,
a jaded record was playing a trashy ballad

—bitter parody of lost paradise
with your unhealthy light!
Ends of weeks, long like a trailing dress,
the lighthouse bathed us, abandoned boats
women were there, from every land,
pieces of meat with a rose in their hair
love was according to race,
sailors had passed through, and dockworkers,
violence had passed through, and bad luck,
smokestacks had blasted their horns in their skins
riggings had snagged in their hair
what voyages! with the storm and the swell,
those breasts, heavy and oily, smelled
of pink cow piss and faraway mothers
the sweet-smelling skin of little sisters bloomed there
delicate flesh, flesh of sisters, of mothers,
flesh revered of all flesh
promised lands!

at the ends of life of death—*promised.*

XXVIII

Ça commençait toujours par des prises de vue
des ports que l'on quittait, de foules sur les quais,
et à la fin la mer avait son mot à dire
ou ces choses que nul n'avait photographiées.

La danseuse espagnole se mit à danser tout à coup
au son d'une guitare molle
sur le pont des troisièmes.

Que de nuages! pendant des jours et des semaines . . .
Si tout à coup quelqu'un criait: TERRE
—nous aurait-elle oubliés?

Que d'eau! pendant des jours et des semaines!

La danseuse espagnole dansait sur le tropique
quelque danse du clan primitif, magique,
faite tout simplement pour apaiser les morts.

Ce fut à l'Équateur quand la chaleur monta
que sa danse devint irritante.
On était las du mouvement.

Ce fut, bien sûr, le mal du pays qu'au début
elle dansa. Et puis la crainte
de ces pays où l'on s'enfonçait tous les jours
qui prenaient possession de vous sans être là
rouges et noirs
avec des hommes vifs et des serpents paresseux
des palmes décevantes
et soudain on eût dit que ce n'était plus ça,
on entrait à sa suite dans un torrent à truites
puis la saison muait
c'était la fièvre des coloniaux, le délire,
la fièvre verte,
puis enfin quelque chose de pur, de robes blanches

XXVIII

It always began the same, with a wide shot
of ports as we departed, crowds on the docks,
and by the end the sea had gotten its word in
such things as no one has ever photographed.

The Spanish dancer suddenly started dancing
to the sound of a languid guitar
on the third-class deck.

Only clouds! for days and weeks on end . . .
If someone had suddenly shouted: LAND
—would she have forgotten us?

Only water! for days and weeks on end!

The Spanish dancer danced across the tropics
some primitive, magic dance of the clan
invented simply to pacify the dead.

Near the equator, when the heat rose,
her dance became an irritation.
We were tired of movement.

At first, of course, it was homesickness
she danced. And then the fear
of those new countries we made for day by day
that took possession of you even from far
red and black
with fierce men and listless snakes
and deceptive palms
and suddenly it seemed it wasn't that anymore,
we followed her into a rushing trout stream
then the season changed
to colonial fevers, delirium,
green fever,
then finally something pure, white robes,

une limpidité de roc, d'enfance lisse,
de rêves sans matière,
de pur vertige, ah!
Le pont tournait, tournait
c'était cruel, c'était inhumain, c'était lâche,
on se pinçait pour voir si on était éveillé
même les matelots n'osaient pas traverser la musique,
ils avaient peur de la crotter
ils se sentaient gênés d'être vivants et lourds
d'avoir des testicules et de fumer la pipe.

Ce fut alors qu'avec des lenteurs de boas,
orteil après orteil, pièce par pièce,
les émigrants se levèrent au grand étonnement
de leurs femmes enceintes
brusquement ils sentirent que le temps coulait
qui n'allait pas revenir,
qu'il fallait faire quelque chose
tricher au jeu, jurer, sangloter, se saouler
ou noyer dans le sang

l'affreuse cruauté de la joie parfaite.

a clarity of stone, untroubled childhood,
ineffable dreams,
pure vertigo, ah!
The deck spun and spun
it was cruel, it was inhuman, it was cowardly,
we pinched ourselves to check if we were awake
even the sailors dared not cross the music,
afraid of muddying it
they felt ashamed of being alive and heavy,
of having testicles and smoking a pipe.

It was then, as slowly as a boa,
joint by joint, piece by piece,
the emigrants rose to the great surprise
of their pregnant wives
abruptly they felt that time was flying
and would not return,
they had to do something,
cheat at cards, swear, sob, get drunk
or drown in blood

the terrible cruelty of perfect joy.

XXIX

C'est une voix qui crie dans le désert «où suis-je?»
Hier, c'était l'océan, la nausée,
et l'envie d'une terre solide dans la paume—
la terre!
Mais aujourd'hui le jour avance dans le brouillard
haletant. Sur le pont, des marins de brouillard
s'enchevêtrent. On ne sait où le bateau commence
où il finit. Un pas de plus c'est le chaos.
La sirène gémit, hurle,
elle crie dans le désert «je suis là, je suis là»
et l'écho lui répond «je suis là, je suis là!»
Attention à ma vie. Elle est fragile. Oh! comme
elle est fragile. Et pourtant si pleine de sa soif.
Je me penche sur mon passé—rien; sur mon avenir—rien.
Je te cherche, où es-tu? une femme de brouillard entre autres.
Que de fantômes, pour vivre, ai-je trahi? Je ne sais.
Leur sang coule. Où sont les vivants? Du brouillard.
On voudrait s'accrocher à quelque épave, corde,
canot, désir, noyé, chevelure, espoir . . .
Mais le bateau avance haletant, il a peur,
il a peur de la vie, il a peur de lui-même,
il ne sait d'où il vient, il ne sait où il va
c'est une voix qui crie . . .
                    L'entends-tu comme elle crie
dans le désert?

XXIX

Now a voice that calls in the desert, "Where am I?"
Yesterday, the ocean, nausea,
the desire to hold in the palm dry land—
dry land!
But today the day advances through panting
fog. On deck, the sailors of fog
overlap. It's not clear where the boat begins
or ends. One step farther, and chaos.
The foghorn howls and moans,
calls in the desert, "I am here, I am here!"
and the echo replies, "I am here, I am here!"
Careful there with my life. It is fragile. Oh, it is
so fragile. And yet so full of its thirst.
I lean close to my past—nothing; to my future—nothing.
I seek you, where are you? Just one more woman of fog.
How many ghosts, to live, did I betray? I do not know.
Their blood is flowing. Where are the living? All fog.
We need to grab at some piece of debris, or rope
or lifeboat, desire, drowned body, floating hair, hope . . .
But the boat sails on, panting, afraid,
afraid of life, afraid of itself,
unsure where it comes from, unsure where it's going.
Only a voice that calls . . .
                              Do you hear how it calls
in the desert?

XXX

Et puisque la tempête m'y jette, c'est une île!
Une île sans chemise, légère comme un cil,
une île déjà vue; ni mère; ni nourrice . . .
Que la terre est petite!
                    —Eh quoi! c'est toi, Ulysse?
Qu'es-tu allé chercher dans un pays pareil?
—J'avais sommeil!
                    —Eh bien! couche-toi. Le sommeil
est chaud comme le sang du cochon dans l'étable
Est-ce ton ombre—ou toi—qui s'est assise à table?
—J'avais faim. Trop de mers, de vase et de nausée . . .
—Désastre d'un destin si longuement osé!
Te voilà, tel qu'au port le fleuve te charrie,
vieux cheval de retour, viande de boucherie,
esprit vaincu! Le creux s'est emparé du fruit!

—Il sonne, plein encor de tout ce qui le fuit!
—Ô son, à peine lourd du vide qu'il dénonce,
tais-toi, tais-toi chanson de l'homme qui renonce!
Si lasse que ta soif soit d'elle-même, enfin
craindrait-elle? . . . —Qui sait la chose que je crains?
—Tant pis, sur les écueils, si le vieux meuble craque!

. . . Mouettes au cœur de sel! Nuages de l'Ithaque! . . .

XXX

And since the gale has flung me here, it's an island!
An island without a shirt on, light as an eyelash,
an island I've seen before; not mother, not nurse . . .
The earth is so small!
                                    —Well, well, Ulysses, is that you?
What brings you to such a land?
—I felt so sleepy!
                                    —In that case, sleep. For sleep
is warm like the blood of pigs in the sty
Is that your shadow—or you—that sits down to eat?
—I was hungry. Too many seas, and nausea and silt . . .
—What wreck of a fate so fearlessly pursued!
Look at you, as the river drags you through port,
old lag fit for the butcher
defeated spirit! The void made off with the fruit!

—It rings, still full of all that flees it!
—O note, without the weight of the void it decries,
be quiet, be quiet, song of the man who has renounced!
However tired your thirst may be of itself, still,
could it be scared? . . . —Who knows the thing I fear?
—Too bad, if the ancient wardrobe breaks on the reef!

. . . Salt-hearted gulls! Clouds of Ithaca! . . .

XXXI

de la mort à la mort
nous sommes passés de main à main, de bouche à bouche,
de regard à regard,
de main à main, pauvre fausse monnaie,
de bouche à bouche, pauvre fausse parole,
par les mains de l'eau fraîche
nous sommes descendus jusqu'au sommeil des poissons,
notre chemise séchait sur le sable avec les ourlets des méduses,
—elles avaient été transparentes!
De regard à regard nous avons usé notre trame,
les mites ont mangé, pure laine, nos âmes,
et notre éternité elle-même, oh notre
éternité, a fait de l'eau comme un canot
plein d'eau verte, de feuilles jaunies et de silence
qui craque.
          Eh bien! vas-y, craque vieux cœur. Est-il,
est-il encore main qui puisse remailler
l'irréparable? Ô, mains fuyantes, mains de femmes!
—nous avons perdu pied dans le regard des femmes
—elles avaient été transparentes!
De la mort à la mort ce n'est qu'une chanson,
on s'en lave les dents et la bouche
  . . . Que cherches-tu dans la mémoire,
une chanson, un fruit qui fond dans la mémoire,
un fruit, rien qu'un fruit,
une chanson qui hait la vie,
la vie, la vie comptée de la mort à la mort,
cachée dans les bas de laine ou payée au comptant,
notre vie à nous tous, notre propre vie,
ma vie à moi plus importante que la vôtre,
ma vie à moi, comprenez-vous?
une chanson qui monte de mes propres entrailles,
une chanson et qui m'étouffe,

XXXI

from death to death
we passed from hand to hand, from mouth to mouth,
from gaze to gaze,
from hand to hand, poor counterfeits,
from mouth to mouth, poor broken word,
we dove through the hands of the cold water
to reach the sleep of the fishes,
our shirt dried on the sand beside the hems of the jellyfish
—they had been transparent!
From gaze to gaze we wore out our thread,
moths ate holes in our souls, pure wool,
and our eternity itself, oh our
eternity, took on water like a rowboat full
of green water, yellowed leaves and cracking
silence.
            Well, then, go on and crack, old heart. Are there
still hands that can mend the weave
of the irreparable? O fleeing hands, women's hands!
—we lost our footing in the gaze of women
—they had been transparent!
From death to death is only a song,
we use it to wash our teeth and mouths
 . . . What are you looking for in memory,
a song, a fruit that melts in memory,
a fruit, only a fruit,
a song that hates this life,
this life, this life reckoned from death to death,
stashed in wool stockings or paid in cash,
everyone's lives, our own lives,
my own life more important than yours,
my own life, you understand?
a song that rises from my gut,
a song, and one that chokes me

et qui se troue au fur et à mesure qu'on la chante,
qui s'épuise et qui fond dans une bouche d'égout
—au fur et à mesure!

that as we go on wears full of holes,
wears out and melts in the sewer's mouth
—as we go on!

XXXII

et cependant les choses sont là, les mêmes choses,
ou à peu près les mêmes.
À peine le regard un peu vieilli dans la tension du visage.
À peine le ressort a-t-il cédé un peu
dans le pli douloureux de la bouche vaincue . . .
Les méridiens tracés à la craie sur le globe
comme toujours traversent le rein du matelot
qui chante, pour tromper la faim de son angoisse.
. . . On songe à une bête et plate indifférence
enceinte d'un bonheur rugueux, et qui s'ignore,
longue maternité d'un infini blessé
qui tombe à terre.
À peine un bruit de conscience
et un langage à peine.
Je m'avance et je sens tinter le poids léger du monde
dans mes mains.
«Lourde légèreté.» Que la balance est juste
entre réel et songe, entre la soif et l'eau!
Quelle tendresse exacte sépare l'immobile
du mouvement et quel dieu cueille au-dedans de nous
cette prière—ou cette absence de prière?

XXXII

yet things are there, the same things,
or nearly the same.
The gaze just slightly aged in the strain of the face.
The spring just slightly relaxed
in the painful fold of the defeated mouth . . .
The meridians traced on the globe in chalk
still cross the small of the back of the sailor
who sings to trick the hunger of his dread.
. . . We dream of a simple, plain indifference
round with a rugged joy, unaware of itself,
the long pregnancy of a wounded infinite
that falls to the ground.
Hardly a sound of conscience
hardly a language.
I advance and hear the world's slight weight
chime in my hands.
"Weighty lightness." The scale is so true
between reality and dream, between water and thirst!
What tenderness is it that separates the immobile
from movement, what god gathers in us
this prayer—or this absence of prayer?

XXXIII

Quand nous entrâmes dans le port
il y avait des milliers de vivants et quelques morts
que l'on portait au loin, hors de la ville.
Mais le port était si tranquille,
si transparent et si doré,
que rien n'y paraissait taré,
si bien que l'on eût dit que ces morts à la manque
avaient eu tort de ne pas se mêler aux vivants
sur la place des Fêtes où, jusqu'au soir tombant,
l'écuyère montée sur un cheval savant
traversa les cerceaux de feu des saltimbanques.

XXXIII

When we entered port
there were thousands of living souls and a few dead
that were carried far, outside of town.
But the port was so calm,
transparent and limned with gold,
it seemed that nothing there was flawed,
and you would have said those would-be dead
were wrong to keep apart from the living
on the Public Square, where as evening fell
the rider mounted on her circus horse
leaped through the rings of fire of the acrobats.

XXXIV

Il fut un temps, camarades,
où nos pieds enfonçaient dans la terre comme le fer à charrue,
la sève nous prenait pour un arbre, y montait
les oiseaux nous prenaient pour des toits, s'y nichaient,
et la femme venait à nous, nous prendre la semence
pour en faire je ne sais quoi—
Étions-nous donc des dieux?

Il fut un temps, camarades,
où le sanglot des hommes monta jusqu'à nos reins
le fruit était-il donc véreux?
le mal était-il incurable?
Ah, il fallait jeter des ponts sur les rivières
arracher le secret aux herbes, aux entrailles
des choses—
inventer, oublier des quantités de choses!
Si ce monde est mauvais que de mondes
à naître! Nous y pourvoirons.

Il fut un temps, camarades,
où nous nous sommes usés au monde,
où nos regards en y entrant se sont tordus comme clous
la vieillesse, la solitude,
savez-vous ce que c'est? et l'affreuse nouvelle
qu'on meurt sur les saisons?
Allez, allez, il faut s'agripper à la vie!
Et la vie s'est effondrée comme un plancher pourri
et la noce des jours est tombée dans la cave
avec ses musiciens aveugles . . .

Je ne songeais pas, camarades,
qu'un jour nous referions ce voyage d'Ulysse
les bourses vides. Il fut un temps
où nous ne songions pas que notre soif des hommes
et notre soif d'éternité

XXXIV

Comrades, there was a time
when our feet sank in the earth like the plow's iron,
sap mistook us for trees and rose in us
birds mistook us for roofs and made their nests there
and woman approached to take our seed
to do with it who knows what—
Were we gods?

Comrades, there was a time
when the sob of man rose to the small of our backs
so was the fruit diseased?
was the ill incurable?
Ah, we had to span the rivers with bridges
to tear the secrets from herbs, from the gut
of things—
invent and forget such quantities of things!
If this world is evil, what about worlds
to come? We will provide for them.

Comrades, there was a time
when we wore ourselves down in the world,
when our gaze, as it entered, bent like a nail
old age, solitude,
do you know what those are? and the awful news that
according to the seasons we die?
Come on, come on, we must hold onto life!
And life collapsed like a rotten floorboard
and the wedding of days fell into the cellar
with the blind musicians . . .

Comrades, I never dreamed
one day we would repeat the voyage of Ulysses
with empty pockets. There was a time
we wouldn't have dreamed our thirst for men
our thirst for eternity

ne feraient plus qu'une poignée
de fiente, à peine chaude
—d'oiseaux.

would amount in the end to a handful
of bird droppings
—barely warm.

XXXV

Ce ne sont pas pourtant des visions d'insomnie.
Je veux! Les îles sont en marche.
Je veux! Voici le sang ancien revenu,
les villes et leurs bannières.
Je veux! Voici le pain quotidien qui pousse
sur mon commandement
dans les antiques lois et les terres en friche.
Je fais jaillir du blé dans les vieux marbres morts
des roses dans les vieilles bibles . . .
—Oh! l'homme beau sur tout cela,
l'homme puissant et qui décide et qui peut tout
—un homme, pas un songe!
—un homme, pas une voix éraillée!
—un homme sans genoux, qui chante
et que rien ne peut balayer de la terre
(pendant qu'il chante)
comme une feuille morte en la saison des loups.

XXXV

Yet these are not the visions of sleepless nights.
I want! The islands are on the move.
I want! Behold, the ancient blood has returned,
cities and their pennants.
I want! Behold, the daily bread that grows
at my command
in the ancient laws and abandoned fields.
I make wheat burst forth between dead marble tombs
and roses in old Bibles . . .
—Oh! and man beautiful through all this
man who is powerful, who chooses, who can do anything
—a man, not a dream!
—a man, not a rasping voice!
—a man without knees, who sings
and whom nothing can sweep from the earth
(as long as he sings)
like a dead leaf in the season of wolves.

XXXVI

À la fin, quand la mer
comptera les navires qui ont coulé à pic
dans sa bouche sans fond,
quelle fête pour tous les gosses de poissons!
Mais quand ils seront là, tendus sur leurs arêtes,
—laissez-moi m'en aller!

À la fin, quand le sol
comptera tous les hommes qui y sont descendus
sans se faire prier,
quel long communiqué de victoire à crier
aux rescapés des îles basses.
Oh! le parfum de rhum, de mort et de mélasse
—d'esclaves!

Oui, nous avons trop bu!
La mer danse déjà dans nos regards, le sol
tangue. On nous a trop vus.
Ça sent le discours de la lave . . .
Qu'ils comptent leurs vaincus!
chassez l'odeur nue de l'esclave!
Ils ne nous auront pas à genoux, nous sommes
au-delà de la force, des lois
. . . ivres morts!

XXXVI

At the end, when the sea
will count the ships that went straight down
in its bottomless mouth,
what a party for all the fishes' kids!
But when they're all there, stretched on their bones,
—let me go!

At the end, when the ground
will count the men who went down into its dark
without needing to be asked,
what long-winded victory proclamation to shout
to the survivors of the atolls.
Oh! the odor of rum, molasses and death
—of slaves!

Yes, we have drunk too much!
The sea dances already in our eyes, the ground
pitches. We have been seen, too much.
It reeks of the lava's discourse . . .
Let them count their captives!
dispel the naked smell of slaves.
They will never have us on our knees, we are
beyond all force, and laws
. . . dead drunk!

XXXVII

à Léon Chestov

Peu importe la vue qui voit mais que ne fouette la vision,
qui voit mais ne peut pas mordre à même le monde,
peu importe l'esprit qui n'a soif que de soi
qui bascule au tangage, que le roulis jette à terre,
mais qui ne peut incliner l'axe de l'océan
ni découvrir un monde
craignant de rien changer au sens des Écritures
frêle esprit accroché à sa vie et tirant,
essayant de traîner sa vie dans sa mort
pareil aux bateliers
de la Volga, halant depuis la berge, les
gros chalands avançant dans les remous du fleuve!

Peu importe les fleuves
à ceux pour qui la vie est de la terre ferme,
tranquillement assis aux terrasses chauffées,
j'ai vu l'eau soulevée monter à leurs épaules
elle trempait leur cœur, moisissait leurs poumons
j'ai vu et j'ai crié «au secours»
j'avais déjà crié aux premiers jours du monde
vais-je crier ainsi jusqu'à la fin du monde
j'ai vu tant de vivants devenus tout à coup
des morts et tant de morts
jeter leur ligne aux eaux poisseuses de la vie
tant de sources auxquelles avaient collé mes lèvres
sans soif et tant de soifs restées inapaisées,
tant d'ombres, tant de limbes,
que j'ai souvent frappé sur la table et crié
«À quoi bon tout cela?»
Que savions-nous si le matin était réel
le grand matin des hommes,
et leur soleil que l'on se partageait saignant

XXXVII

for Lev Shestov

Sight that sees but is not lashed by vision means nothing,
that sees but cannot bite straight to the world,
the spirit thirsting only for itself means nothing,
that falls at the pitching deck, that the swell throws to the ground,
but that cannot tilt the ocean's axis
or discover a world
afraid of changing the meaning of Scripture
weak spirit gripping its life and pulling,
trying to drag its life into its death
like Volga
boatmen who guide from the shore the
great barges advancing in the eddying river!

Rivers mean nothing
to those who think that life belongs on dry land,
comfortably seated on the heated terrace of a café,
I saw the rising water reach their shoulders
it wet their hearts, mildewed their lungs
I saw and I shouted "help"
I had shouted already in the first days of the world
will I be shouting until the end of the world
I saw so many of the living all of a sudden become
the dead and so many dead
cast their lines in the murky waters of life
so many springs to which I pressed my lips
without thirst, and so many thirsts that remained unquenched,
so many shades, so many limbos,
that often I bang on the table and shout
"What is the use of all this?"
How could we know if the morning was real
the great morning of men,
and the sun we shared dripping red

était-il vrai, était-il faux,
à quoi bon tant de navigateurs, de périples,
de continents nouveaux, de paradis perdus,
de panoplies, de consciences,
où traînent leur ennui les princes de l'exil
parmi des souvenirs de cors et de tueries?
Assez, assez mon insomnie!
Le monde est là peut-être, mais suis-je bien en lui?
Je passe et il ne reste rien dans le miroir,
pas même un trou
et j'ai beau m'exercer sur les mots hors d'usage
comme on redresse au marteau les clous qui ont déjà
servi, tordus, et qu'on les enfonce à nouveau,
il n'est pas de chanson donnée à tout le monde,
je ne peux pas fermer les yeux,
je dois crier toujours jusqu'à la fin du monde:
«il ne faut pas dormir jusqu'à la fin du monde»
—je ne suis qu'un témoin.

was it real, was it fake,
what use all these explorers and voyages,
new continents, paradises lost,
great collections, consciousness
where princes of exile drag their weariness
amid memories of bugle calls and slaughters?
Enough, my insomnia, enough!
The world may be there, but am I there in the world?
I pass, and nothing remains in the mirror,
not even a hole
and for all I practice old-fashioned words
as a hammer is used to straighten bent
nails and knock them in again,
there is not a song for everyone,
I cannot close my eyes,
I must shout until the end of the world:
"you must not sleep until the end of the world"
—I am only a witness.

XXXVIII

Quel pavillon, jadis, flotta sur cette hampe
un peu de sel aux lèvres, une amertume au lit.
Vas-tu vomir enfin ton âcre mort, coolie?
La vie ça te connaît comme une vieille crampe.

La Terre quelque part. C'est la même folie
et la même insomnie . . . et c'est la même lampe.
Oh! finir proprement en un coin de l'estampe.
Et que le vent t'emporte, duvet du pissenlit . . .

Non, ce n'est rien . . . Pitié des hommes. Et de moi-même!
Je n'ai plus que mon sang pour t'allaiter, poème . . .
Tu es si lasse, ô voix qui crie dans les déserts.

Mon cœur est-il vraiment trop lourd pour ces vendanges?
Meurt-on sans le savoir sur la cuisse des anges?
Dieu, dans sa propre nuit, a-t-il les yeux ouverts?

XXXVIII

What colors flew above this flagpole once,
with salty lips, in bed an old regret?
Coolie, will you vomit up at last
your bitter death? You know life like an old cramp.

Somewhere, the Earth. Always the same madness,
the same insomnia . . . and the same lamp.
Oh! for a decent end in a corner of the print.
May the wind take you, dandelion seed . . .

But no, it's nothing . . . Pity men. And myself!
I've nothing left but my blood to nurse you, poem . . .
You are so tired, O voice that calls in the desert.

So is my heart too heavy for these harvests?
Do we die unknowing on the angels' thigh?
Are God's eyes open in his private night?

XXXIX

Ulysse, il nous faudra nous quitter; la terre cesse . . .
Les rats, depuis longtemps, nous ont rongé les cordes,
et les mouettes picoré la cire de nos oreilles—

Liés par nous-mêmes, c'est trop!

Veux-tu que l'on se jette à la mer—librement?

J'ai hâte d'écouter la chanson qui tue! . . .

XXXIX

Ulysses, it's time to part; the earth has come to an end . . .
The rats have long gnawed through our ropes,
and seagulls pecked the wax from our ears—

Bound by ourselves, now really, that's too much!

Shall we throw ourselves into the sea—of our own free will?

I'm dying to hear the fatal melody! . . .

Selected Bibliography

Works of Fondane in English Translation

Cinepoems and Others. Edited by Leonard Schwartz. New York: New York Review of Books, 2016.

Existential Monday: Philosophical Essays. Edited, introduced, and translated from the French by Bruce Baugh. New York: New York Review of Books, 2016.

Works of Fondane, Modern Editions

Baudelaire et l'expérience du gouffre. Brussels: Complexe, 1994. (Original edition: Seghers, 1947.)

La Conscience malheureuse. Edited by Olivier Salazar-Ferrer. Paris: Verdier, 2013. (Original edition: Denoël et Steele, 1936.)

Écrits pour le cinéma: Le muet et le parlant. Edited by Michel Carassou, Olivier Salazar-Ferrer, and Ramona Fotiade. Paris: Verdier, 2007.

Faux traité d'esthétique: Essai sur la crise de réalité. Paris: Paris-Méditerranée, 1998. (Original edition: Denoël, 1938.)

Le Lundi existentiel et le dimanche de l'histoire. Monaco: Editions du Rocher, 1990. (Original edition: in *Existence*, edited by Jean Grenier, Gallimard, 1945.)

Le Mal de fantômes. Edited by Patrice Beray and Michel Carassou. Paris: Verdier, 2006.

Poèmes retrouvés, 1925–1944: Edition sans fin. Edited by Monique Jutrin. Paris: Parole et Silence, 2013.

Rencontres avec Léon Chestov. Edited by Nathalie Baranoff and Michel Carassou. Paris: Non Lieu, 2016.

Rimbaud le voyou. Paris: Non Lieu, 2010. (Original edition: Denoël et Steele, 1933.)

Théâtre complet. Edited by Eric Freedman. Paris: Non Lieu, 2012.

Original Editions of Fondane's Poetry

"Au temps du poème et poèmes épars." Edited by Michel Carassou. *Non Lieu* (1978).

L'Exode. N.p.: La Fenêtre Ardente, 1965.

"Le Mal des fantômes." *Cahiers du Sud* 268 (Oct.–Dec. 1944): 121–31.

Titanic. Brussels: Cahiers du Journal des Poètes, 1937.

Trois scenarii: Ciné-poèmes. Paris: Documents Internationaux de l'Esprit Nouveau, 1928.

Ulysse. Brussels: Cahiers du Journal des Poètes, 1933.

Selected Critical Works

Benjamin Fondane: Roumanie, Paris, Auschwitz. Paris: Non Lieu and Mémorial de la Shoah, 2010.

Beray, Patrice. *Benjamin Fondane, au temps du poème.* Paris: Verdier, 2006.

Escomel, Gloria. "B. Fondane et G. Gaucher: 'Des liens au-dessus du temps.'" *Cahiers Benjamin Fondane* 1 (1997): 30–48.

Gruson, Claire. "Poésie et mémoire dans *Ulysse.*" *Cahiers Benjamin Fondane* 11 (2008): 130–41.

Jutrin, Monique. *Benjamin Fondane; ou, Le Périple d'Ulysse.* Paris: Nizet, 1989.

———. "Du mal d'Ulysse au mal des fantômes." *Cahiers Benjamin Fondane* 11 (2008): 117–29.

Kafka, Franz. *Diaries, 1910–1923.* Translated by Martin Greenberg with Hannah Arendt. New York: Shocken, 1988.

Namenwirth, Evelyne. "Marseille–Buenos Aires: Reportage d'Ernest Claes." *Cahiers Benjamin Fondane* 11 (2008): 142–52.

Nirenberg, Ricardo. "Benjamin Fondane et Victoria Ocampo." *Cahiers Benjamin Fondane* 1 (1997): 6–18.

Salazar-Ferrer, Olivier. *Benjamin Fondane.* Escalquens: Oxus, 2004.

———. *Benjamin Fondane et la révolte existentielle.* Clichy: Courlevour, 2007.

van Sevenant, Ann. "Disjointedness at Work." *Cahiers Benjamin Fondane* 10 (2007): 48–56.

———. "Fondane et la dualectique." *Titanic* 1 (2013): 5–20.

———. Introduction to *Faux traité d'esthétique*, by Benjamin Fondane. Paris: Paris-Méditerranée, 1998.

Benjamin Fondane (1898–1944) was a Jewish Romanian writer who immigrated to France in 1923, drawn by his love of French poetry and philosophy. Before his untimely death, he published several collections of French poetry as well as philosophical essays reflecting his close relationship with Russian existentialist philosopher Lev Shestov. Selections of his work have been translated into English, notably in the recent volumes *The Existential Monday* (2016) and *Cinepoems and Others* (2016).

Nathaniel Rudavsky-Brody has translated the work of French and Belgian poets. His translation of Fondane's long poem *The Sorrow of Ghosts* was included in the collection *Cinepoems and Others*, and his selection of Paul Valéry's poetry is forthcoming from Farrar, Straus, and Giroux. His work has also appeared in *TriQuarterly*, *Two Lines*, and *Cerise*, and he is the author of two volumes of poetry in French. In 2013 he was awarded the Susan Sontag Prize for Translation.